AN UNNATURAL CHOICE

MARY HODDER ROSS

Mary Hodder Ross
An Unnatural Choice

ISBN: 978-1-9990782-0-1

Manufactured in Canada

Editor: Lori Bamber
Cover and Interior Design: Laura Wrubleski
Publishing Support: The Self Publishing Agency

for my beloved husband
who never once, not for a second,
stopped believing in me
while I tortured and caressed
this story out of me

*mighty stories I hold
in the curve of my hand
in the words breaking free
from the tip of my pen
upon the waiting page
telling my tale
singing my sorrow
forging my faith
unveiling the mystery
of my woman stance
my stormy secrets
my plod upon the earth
looking for Jesus
and salvation
seeking God
and forgiveness
and the holy light
to lead me to grace
and a sacred place
let God be a woman
I say
with a woman's soul
and a woman's crooked
sense of humour
earned by tragedy
and scars that don't heal*

no matter the time that passes

give me space

to tell you who I am

listen now

while I still have the courage

to tell you the truth

because the day may come

when the muse departs

and what I intended to say

will fall silent within my breast

and you will be left to wonder

who I was

and why my life mattered

at all

prologue

Adoption is two sides of a single coin. One side is the gift. The other is sacrifice. I have been flipping that coin for years, the odds always against me.

Bringing my eldest son into the world was a gift. He is a gift to the family that raised him and to me, as I live every day knowing he is in the world because of me. His very name means "gift."

Sacrifice is the other, rougher side of the coin. Loss, pain and relinquishment. It is about struggling with regret and never being able to change my decision. It is about wanting to go back in time and rewrite the story, keep my son and be his mother every single day of his life. It's about thinking that no other woman, no matter who she is, could ever love him the way I love him. It's about a cry deep within me that is rarely heard by anyone else but is sometimes the only thing I can hear. It is about walking around in the world feeling less than whole, about waking up from dreams in the dark night, my arms aching and grasping. It is about the life I live as a birth mother, my mother-not-mother existence.

Sacrifice. It is the side of the coin where I live. It has been my secret, my defining, largely untold story. Life altered, path diverging, world shattered—never to be fully reconstructed.

No matter how much I want to flip the coin to the side of the gift, it always, invariably, lands on the side of sacrifice.

Since 1982, I've written my story on pieces of paper, in journals and in various electronic documents that I intended to "get back to someday." I have shared bits of it with women in living rooms and offices, haphazard conversations where we found meaning in our shared experiences. I have told it to myself in various wounded states of mind when I went looking for the parts of me that I keep hidden from the world. It has been easier to deny, and when necessary, to lie. I told myself that I did the right thing, the best thing, the only possible thing. I repeated this until it was rote, readily recited. Well, not readily. It was my explanation, the justification that allowed me to believe and to convey to others that I was still a good person. A person who sacrificed. A person who might be admired for selflessness. But the truth is that the whole story is not a nice or happy one to relate, but a raw, messy and strangled admission of remorse and irreversible loss.

On a summer evening several years ago, my daughter was in Africa on a volunteer mission, and her younger brother was in Arizona celebrating his recent graduation from high school. I missed them both and was thinking about how quickly they had grown. All those seemingly endless years of togetherness under the same roof every day had suddenly come to an end. Mornings preparing for school, evenings of homework, good night snuggles and stories—done. But I realized, too, that the love we share strongly connects us even in our absence from one another. Physical presence is not required to sustain our bond.

They were both far from me and yet with me; I was with them.

Dusk fell over downtown Vancouver as I looked out my bedroom window. The fading day and edge of night overlapped as interior lights reshaped buildings into a soft glow against the North Shore Mountains. My thoughts returned, as they do, to the son I gave up, his name on my lips. I felt hot, flushed and faint; the air grew thick around me. Trying to breathe, unable to sit or stand, I leaned against my bed until wails of suppressed sadness erupted and were surely heard on the street twenty-one floors below. I slumped to the floor, sorrow pouring out of me in unstoppable, wrenching waves as it had so many times before. The sorrow I otherwise held in, every day.

He is the son that I love in total absentia. Does he feel connected to me in any way? Am I connected to him?

Giving up my son was not the right thing or the best thing. Not for me. It was not the only possible thing I could have done. It was the choice I made, the choice I live with, and the choice I suffer. The years of not knowing him, not touching him, not being his mother—those years can never be recovered.

I sat on the floor in my sweaty, crumpled dress with my hair wild about my head, my face flushed and my throat sore, sobs slowly subsiding. I leaned on the side of my bed and closed my eyes.

I want to believe that love transcends space and time and distance, but I was bereft, thinking again that my absence might be nothing but absence to him. I want to believe that he feels my love. Not in the usual filial, day-to-day sense but in spirit and heart, a transcendent arc across distance and time. It is the hope that has sustained me in the day after day after day that I have lived without him. Sadly, on that evening, like so many others, the hope remained abstract, an unanswered call.

This is the story that defines me. A woman of secrets—hard to reach and harder to understand; a woman whose relationships were fractured because I came into them feeling less than whole. Walking around inside a carefully constructed facade, I hoped that if I fooled others, I could fool myself too.

I am a woman who spent much of my life sure that happiness would evade me because I didn't deserve it.

I tell my story now for the two children I raised, who I love dearly and who have seen but not always understood my sadness, indecision and failings. I tell it for my mother, who persistently encouraged me to write this book and find the grandson she never got to meet. I tell it for my family, who did not know about the son I gave up until I wrote a letter to them revealing my long-held secret on his thirtieth birthday.

I tell it for the women along my path—past, present and future—women who shelter stories similar to mine. I tell it for myself, so that I may reclaim peace and live more openly and fully. But I tell it mostly for my firstborn son, desperately wanted yet given up to adoption, so that one day he may hold this book in his hands. It is my expression of gratitude for his life and my testament of love for him, even if he does not feel wanted and loved by me. It is his history and beginning, the one only I can reveal.

I've tried to preserve the facts and circumstances as they occurred. Where my memories are vague, I admit it. I mean no harm to others. My sincere desire is to tell my version of events, remaining close to my own experiences and the way they affected me.

My intent is to shine a light on the experience of birth mothers, other women with their own stories, all deeply personal and painful. Too many of us remain silent, sad and alone. We each made a choice that became pivotal to our ever after. By sharing my truth, I hope to ignite conversations and diminish the shame that burdens us.

Adoption is often seen as a "happy ever after" tale of a family who gets the baby they longed for and a baby who gets a better life. It is easier to overlook the birth mother and her regret, guilt and shame. It is more comfortable to focus on the sweet infants surrendered than the hurting teenagers and young adults who struggle with why their birth parents gave them up, who they are and why it is that they can't fill the void they feel in their life. We want to believe that everyone got what they wanted and what was best. But that is not often, maybe never, the case.

Within these pages, I risk vulnerability. My silence and secrets have not served me. My decision cannot be changed and, while I have tried to leave the past alone, it remains urgent. If I am thought senti-mental, I am prepared for that—there is nothing anyone could say that might be worse than the things I have said to myself. My hope is that this book will encourage us all to be more real, for ourselves and for one another. My dream is that judgement will end, and that acceptance will foster understanding.

Who does not have regret? Who does not have a story they would tell if it meant they could be free and happy? This is my desire for my son and, yes, for me. That we be free. Free from the void of the unknown and unanswered, from the hollowness of forever wondering.

It takes courage to give up a child for adoption. It takes courage to live with being adopted. It takes courage to be adoptive parents. Without knowing one another or understanding our individual parts in a complex, emotional and enduring saga, we are together in an extraordinary undertaking.

There can be no peace until we come together. So, yet again, I am flipping the coin: The gift. Sacrifice.

Will the weight of these words finally turn the odds in my favour?

Mom and me, circa 1964
Bowering Park, St. John's, Newfoundland

I tell this story in honour of my mother,
whose hand still holds my heart.

*Mary, Mary, quite contrary,
how does your garden grow?
With silver bells, and cockle shells,
and pretty maids all in a row.*

English nursery rhyme

she sits alone on a swing
legs dangling
toes brushing the ground
arms hanging loose
on either side of the swing's ropes
her head leaning forward
as she watches the sunlight
sparkle through her curls
and gently pushes herself back and forth
with the tiptoe of her red jelly shoes
her orange cotton dress covers her knees
her favourite dress with a giraffe up one side
she wears it often
it makes her smile
she hears a bird singing in a tree nearby
his song, "sweet summer, sweet summer"
lulls her and makes her drowsy
she closes her eyes and drifts
in the distance
she hears other children laughing as they play
she looks up slowly
squinting into the sunlight
but does not see them
just as well
she prefers to stay on the swing
lost in the lazy motion
the soft breeze
and the warm sun
on an afternoon when she is small
untouched by all
the struggles yet to come

a girl of the '60s and '70s

I was born in 1961 at the Cottage Hospital in Burin, Newfoundland. I was almost ten pounds at birth, which is remarkable to me as I am small in frame, as was my mother. More remarkable though were the generous curls on my infant head. My mother said she could twist them into ringlets with her fingers, and indeed there are photographs to prove it. I was child number five, with three brothers and a sister. My younger sister came along when I was five, usurping my status as the youngest, for which I joke I have been unable to forgive her ever since. She and I grew up together, somewhat apart from our much older four siblings.

Until I was six, we lived in a style of house called a saltbox, four square sides, two stories high, uniform rectangular windows up and down, a porch at the kitchen entrance and a back door at the rear. My father built the house soon after he and my mother were married, a wedding present. My mother was anxious to move away from her in-laws, into their own space. The house tucked into a hill on a small patch of land at the end of a long laneway, on the inlet that separated Creston North (our community) from Creston South (or "the other side," as my family referred to it in a somewhat condescending tone). The only way across the inlet at the time was the Canning Bridge in Marystown, the mostly Catholic town that was the centre of shopping, medical care and business. Creston North and Creston South were made up of primarily Protestant residents—United Church, Salvation Army, Pentecostal. Thus it was that my early view of the world was defined by boundaries of land, water and religious segregation.

Tired of the laneway to our house, with less need for our barn and animals after he acquired a permanent job at the Marystown Shipyard, my father attempted to use rollers to move our house to a better location. He chose a place on our land that was along the main road through town, easily accessible year-round. When his roller plan failed, he decided to build a new house instead. He ordered house plans from a home design company in the United States, and I can still see those blueprints spread out on the kitchen table, Mom and Dad leaning over them.

The new house was a bungalow with three bedrooms, a modern home in a place where the traditional Newfoundland saltbox reigned supreme. My dad built it with his own hands, working throughout the evenings and weekends. Sometimes he let me go with him to the site and gave me a small hammer, nails and scrap wood to practice on, telling me to be careful not to hit my fingers. Occasionally I did slam a finger, but it did not stop me. I would wince quietly, for fear I would lose the hammer and nails. I did not become much of a carpenter, although the smell of raw wood remains a favourite. A trip to Home Depot with my husband still takes me back to the memory of my dad and me inside the frame of our growing house, the sun setting and pushing long shadows across the wooden floor.

My father did not borrow money for the house; he paid for everything with cash and built according to his weekly budget. He did not borrow money for anything. Always cash. We moved into the house before the drywall went up so that he could finish building while we lived there. Eventually, he finished the house and then created the driveway, lawn, walkways and flower gardens exactly as they appeared in the drawings. We had a stand-out house in a town where every other house was much the same. My dad joked over the years that he never really got to finish it because each time he thought he was done, my mother came up with another idea it was up to him to execute. It is a credit to their marriage that there was seldom a disagreement between them, at least that we saw. My dad enjoyed nothing more than pleasing his wife. And so, the house grew with us, a collection of stories that revealed my parents' penchant for change and their willingness to make it happen.

My preschool days were spent close to my mother. My earliest memory of her is in the kitchen, in her apron, kneading dough for bread. The smell of it baking in the wood stove comes back to me now, and my mouth waters for the taste of steaming warm bread and butter. My mother would say the treat would spoil dinner, but she invariably relented and let me have a large slice, sometimes two, and joined me in those heavenly moments. I sat beside her on the kitchen daybed, our legs stretched out side by side as we enjoyed our indulgence.

Just us.

While my mother cared for the house and cooking, I busied myself with a host of dolls, teddy bears and tea parties. I took charge of our small living room, talking to my inanimate friends and making them talk to me. I was free to imagine as I pleased. There was no preschool or mom-and-me groups in the 1960s. There was only mom and me, at home. I can still feel the cool of the brightly painted, floral canvas floor beneath my feet. I can feel the stiff fabric of the burgundy chesterfield and chairs.

When I tired of tea parties, I sat my dolls and bears on the wooden stairs that led to the second floor and stood at the bottom, playing mother to my pretend children. Bossy and certain of myself from the start, I was appreciative of any audience, real or imagined, that was willing to listen.

Each Christmas, my dad brought home a big box of Red Delicious apples. The box was layered with soft cardboard trays shaped to hold each apple inside individual apple-shaped grooves. We stored it in the corner of the living room, near the base of the stairs by the back door, where it was coldest. When I played on the stairs, their scent hung sweetly in the air. My dad enjoyed Red Delicious apples his whole life, eating them with pleasure and encouraging the same for us. To this day, whenever I shop for fruit at the market, I look at the bottom of one to see the five points that make a star. I breathe in the scent. A blessed memory of my father and those early Christmas celebrations, when apples were as much a gift for us as any other that we received. My dad said the star at the base of the apple was like the star of Christmas, and that is still how I see it.

In the middle of a typical weekday morning, when it was time, my mother turned on our small black and white television so that I could watch *Romper Room*. Towards the end of each show, Miss Ann said she could see the kids at home through her magic mirror. I sat on my little chair directly in front of the television, but she never said, "I see Mary."

I was disappointed every time. Later I figured that Mary was too plain a name for American television in the 1960s; I felt like my name was a bit of a curse.

In fourth grade, when our teacher said we were to choose a name for French class, I chose Veronique. I thought it marvellously special. I liked the way it sounded and how it felt on my tongue. I carefully wrote each letter across my white name card and placed it on my desk at the start of each French lesson. I did not get to keep the name, but I kept the card for years, stored in a drawer of favourite things.

Having older brothers meant watching westerns on Saturday afternoons and *Hockey Night in Canada* on Saturday nights. While hockey wasn't of interest, I joined them for the westerns as soon as I was old enough. I perched on the back of the armchair, out of the way so no one would be irritated by my presence. I was in love with cowboys, horses and the open plains, where tumbleweeds blew across dusty terrain. I wanted to be a cowboy so badly that my parents eventually got me my own toy holster and guns along with blue cowboy pants and red boots. I never once wanted to be like the girls in those shows. Their shrill screams irritated me and their need to be rescued was unbearable. I am pretty sure that was the inception of my desire to take care of myself. No one need save me: I would do that for myself, thank you very much.

When I was five, I went to kindergarten at a three-room schoolhouse located within walking distance of our home. The first few days my mother walked me to school. After that, my older brother took me, often letting me ride on his shoulders. Soon I was confident enough to walk on my own.

School suited me. I liked the order of rows of seats in the classroom. I adored having my own desk with an attached seat and storage basket under my chair. I inhaled the smell of paper and pencils and crayons, enjoying the feel of them in my hands. I learned to read with the storybooks of *Dick and Jane and Sally*. Those idyllic images of American children with their mom and dad and their pets Puff and Spot inspired my love of reading. The happy, wholesome images lifted them off the page and into my imagination. I was Jane and Spot was my dog.

I vividly recall my first day of kindergarten. On that first morning, my mother twisted my hair into Shirley Temple ringlets with a big yellow satin bow on the top of my head. (She loved giving me that style and I grew to dislike it. One day my mother heard the scissors drop and came running into the kitchen to find a pile of curls in the rocking chair by the stove. The only ringlet remaining was the one I could not reach at the top. She burst into tears and ran out the door. The next day I got to sit in a chair at the hair salon for a pixie cut. I was altogether pleased with myself, despite being in trouble.)

The girl seated in front of me in my kindergarten classroom had a single shiny ponytail with a pink satin bow. She swung that ponytail back and forth, swishing it endlessly across the front of my desk. I wished for a ponytail like that. Then, as we lined up to file out the door for recess, the teacher leaned down to tell me how pretty my hair looked. The girl with the ponytail glared back at me—I could see she wanted the compliment. I had discovered mean girls.

I learned that standing out can be a privilege and a curse. But when you are young, it is mostly a curse. That girl plagued me on the playground and made fun of me, encouraging others to join in. She liked to trip me and push me around.

She laughed hysterically the year that I got a "boy" present at the Santa Claus parade. I use the description "Santa Claus parade" very loosely. It was, more accurately, a very unconvincing "Santa" in the back of a dirty, rusty red pickup truck that roared over the hill and into the cove, arriving with a screeching halt in front of the school where we, a rowdy and excited group of kids, waited anxiously.

Santa yelled out a weak "Ho! Ho! Ho! Merry Christmas!" and then unceremoniously tossed wrapped presents out into the crowd. I don't know who paid for those presents or where they came from, but we desperately wanted them. We stood with upstretched arms and, as soon as we caught a gift, scurried aside to rip off the wrapping and discover what Santa had chosen for us.

That year, Santa chose a truck for me. A truck! Sure enough, Miss Ponytail came running over, flashing her perfect doll in a box. She tugged at the present I was attempting to hide behind discarded Christmas wrap. When she saw my misfortunate, she burst out laughing and yelled for all to hear, "Santa thinks you're a boy!" I hated her. And I hated that stupid Santa who was now exiting quickly up the road in his ugly truck instead of a sleigh. Thankfully, as we walked home, my cousin offered me the storybook he had received in exchange for the truck. I gave it up readily, but I never forgot that moment of humiliation. Miss Ponytail was officially my archnemesis.

In third grade, we were transferred from our community school to an integrated school in the town of Salt Pond. That meant riding a bus. I was sad to leave our schoolhouse with its tiny library, multi-grade classrooms and the gravelled yard where we played hopscotch and tag at recess.

I was especially sad to leave our Christmas concerts, eagerly awaited and well-attended events that were a major part of the celebrations in our small outport town. A Christmas tree was decorated and nestled into the back corner, beside tables set out with Christmas treats and punch to be shared after the concert. We memorized recitations and practiced small skits to perform for the parents and community. The stage seemed large and expansive to me. The audience filled the room, with many people standing along the walls, so full were the seats. On the stage, looking out across the audience, I was excited and proud that my parents were there to see me. My mother, true to form, tied a red ribbon at the top of my ringlets to mark the occasion.

Those primary school days were few, but they remain in my memory as a time of closeness and simple joys, where everything and everyone I knew was within a small circumference of my home, and I did not need anything more.

The integrated school was bigger but not better, and much further from home, meant to eliminate the need for more costly small community schools. Integration brought together kids from every town on the Burin Peninsula, all of us Protestant since the Catholic schools remained outside the integration plan. Each grade had its own classroom. At lunch, we went to a cafeteria to eat the homemade sandwiches and cookies that our mothers prepared and placed inside colourful tin lunchboxes with our apples. At recess, we ran to the playground of swings, slides and seesaws. And at the end of the day, we filed out to the buses for the long ride back home.

The bus stopped directly in front of my house, which served me well in my teen years when I used every second available to perfect my "look" before racing out the door. It was also ideal in winter because I could wait inside until I spotted the other kids emerging from the bus shelter, signalling the bus's arrival. The bus rides were experiences unto themselves. The drone of the engine lulled us back to sleep in the early mornings as we slumped into the seats, not at all anxious to get to school. The afternoon rides were the opposite as we climbed aboard energized by our release from classes.

The bus driver looked anxious in the afternoons, anticipating disruptions that mainly came from the boys. If a fight broke out the bus driver would first yell, "No rampsin' on the bus, boys!" "Rampsin'" was a local term for fighting that never failed to make us giggle behind our hands. If the fight continued, the driver would stomp on the brakes to get their attention. Sometimes he even pulled over and walked down the aisle to separate mischievous boys, who were then forced to ride at the front. It was a hated punishment, as the cool boys rode at the very rear and got away with a lot more than the driver ever saw. (And was most likely grateful to ignore.)

From grade four through to graduation, I rode the bus to school. There were many winter days when the ride was even longer than usual because snow drifts and poor road conditions slowed us down. We talked, laughed, slept and sometimes did homework. We sat with our friends and whispered secrets to one another. We talked about boys while the boys looked through the AC/DC, Alice Cooper and Led Zeppelin records that they lugged under their arms along with their books and assignments. There were no iTunes or iPods or iPhones, of course, not even a Discman or CDs. Just album cover artwork and the songs on the LP to discuss. The bus was our mini world. It was the best and worst of each school day.

We made our way through the latter part of the 1970s with sex, drugs and rock 'n' roll as the backdrop to our youthful climb out of our obscure corner of the world. Kids smoked marijuana at high school dances, hiding behind the bleachers on the soccer field to avoid being discovered by the teachers. Some smoked behind the school during lunch and came back to class with red-rimmed eyes and a weird sense of calm that I almost envied.

Teenage pregnancy was rampant in the 1970s. Kids had sex on Friday nights and sat with their guilt while the minister preached about abstinence as if it were the eleventh commandment on Sunday morning. Our one class on sex education in grade seven, when boys were separated from girls to view the prescribed film on "our bodies," did nothing for our understanding of sex, nor did it prevent our curiosity and hormones from urging us to discover for ourselves.

Birth control was something that loose girls used; abstinence was the choice that good girls made. I did not know many of these "good girls," and there were plenty of pregnant girls, those who had "gotten themselves into trouble." There was no mention of the boys or their part in things. The focus was on the girls who ended up pregnant, wearing their shame publicly as their bellies swelled into full view.

In grade eleven, the 11C class was nicknamed the maternity ward because so many of the girls in that class had gotten "knocked up." Grade eleven was split into A, B and C, with A being the most advanced, B in middle and C the "slow" class. I still find it incredulous that it was arranged in a way that so cruelly labelled some students. I was in the A class, which was an academic and social relief for me, but the injustice of it annoyed me then and annoys me still.

The maternity ward cases crept from C to B and finally to A. I sat in front of a girl whose belly grew large and round, protruding through the opening of her ever-present jean jacket, the last vestige of her teenage composure. She walked around like nothing bothered her, except if she caught you staring at her belly. Then she snapped, "What are you looking at?" As she walked by my desk to go to the pencil sharpener or hand in papers, it made me wonder what it felt like to have a whole other person inside you while you took tests, ran around in gym class, ate lunch in the cafeteria and rode the bus. What would she tell me now, all these years later, when life has changed us both many times over? Would she say that being pregnant in high school was the least of it? Or that it stays with her as a defining experience? I don't know if she had a boy or girl—it was insignificant to me at the time. I was unconcerned and indifferent.

The only female teacher in the school was given the uncomfortable task of talking to the 11C girls about wearing proper maternity clothes. It was winter in Newfoundland and these girls came to school with wool sweaters stretched over their swollen bellies. The male teachers apparently found it unsightly. A sign of the times. The 1970s, the age of sexual revolution—and pregnancy was still considered indecent exposure. Men decided how women should look and imposed their opinions to suit their comfort.

I admit I too was uncomfortable at the time. I was one of the girls who hung out in the hallway to watch the pregnant girls pass. We rolled our eyes and smirked at them. We were cruel and heartless. If I could go back to 1978, I would tell those girls to proudly wear whatever the hell they wanted. I would tell them to shove their bellies into the faces of all those boys who never had to admit or own up to what they had done. I would tell them to walk up to the male teachers and insist they talk to the boys about sexual responsibility. I would pass out birth control like candy, as a statement for choice and freedom. I would proclaim that sex is natural and lovely, not a bad girl's secret.

What was tragic was not that girls got pregnant, but why. Even more tragically, the girls took the blame and endured social exclusion and ridicule. Demonizing birth control limited access to safe sex and personal choices. Cruelly ostracizing girls who got caught had deep and pervasive consequences.

It took me far too long to experience sex as something beautiful because I grew up hearing it was dirty. It also took me far too long to realize that sexual pleasure is as much a woman's domain as a man's—that sex is not a service we perform, not something we permit and abide until it's over.

No one talked openly about it.

Then there was this: one morning when I was about twelve, I was eating my bowl of Captain Crunch while listening to my mother on the telephone. From her side of the conversation, I could tell that the person on the other end was gossiping about some pregnant girl. I marvelled that they said, "got herself pregnant," wondering how girls could do that all on their own. In my mind, that would have made them close to Mary, mother of Jesus, but in my town, they were just harlots. Then my mother said something I would never forget—"If any girl of mine ever comes home pregnant I will disown her." That single sentence held me in the moment like a pin pushed through a piece of paper. Disown me? I was stricken by those words, gagging a bit on my sweet cereal and milk.

My mother was passionate about us having a good education. She devoted herself to making sure that we all got there. She did not want to see pregnancy sideline that dream, as it had for so many others. It was not a time when mothers sat down and talked about sex with their daughters. They were more inclined to use sniffs, tuts and innuendo to make sure we knew it was bad. It was the kind of dissuasion that baffled yet did little to dampen curiosity. My mother's strong reaction on the phone that morning was a reaction to her deepest fear, one that she could not let materialize. But to my young ears, it was a warning that still echoes in my memory.

For me, the things that boys and girls did together when no one else was around just felt strange. Pointless.

I wanted out of my small town. I wanted to be a better person. I wanted education and a means to create my life far beyond the boundaries of the community that had raised me. I looked to the rising roles of women as motivation to move out and up into a world of my own. I wanted some version of Mary Tyler Moore's life—independence, career and sophistication. It was out there, somewhere, and I was going to go get it. I took on leadership roles in high school to expand my abilities—yearbook editor, public speaking, 4H, basketball, and writing contests. I took to leadership naturally. I enjoyed writing and public speaking most of all, and accumulated trophies and awards throughout my high school years.

I refused to learn to type in high school, believing it would set me up as a secretary and I would never get away. My parents had said, "You can always fall back on typing if you are ever without a job." Taking a man's notes by shorthand and typing them was not going to be my fate, so help me God! I wanted to be in charge and have a secretary work for me. My future was vivid and tangible and waiting. Away from my small hometown and marriage and babies pushed along in strollers while dreams disappeared for good.

I was a Newfoundland girl from "around the bay" with dreams that kept me up at night as I willed them to come true. I somehow convinced my parents that I should go to university, even though they'd hoped I'd attend the local trades school and stay close to home. Their approval in place, I sat with friends in our classroom over a lunch period, filling out my application to Memorial University one winter's day. I would be the first in my family to go to university. Most people in my hometown took a trade at the local school, got a job and married soon after. Building a career was not a priority, not even a word that was used or discussed. But I wanted it, a career, something to call my own. I yearned for success and independence.

At the time, high school ended at grade eleven in Newfoundland, a practice that aligned with Great Britain. From kindergarten to high school we sang "God Save the Queen" every morning, along with "O Canada." We stood beside our seats to sing together, immediately following the school announcements over the PA system. It was women like the Queen who inspired hope in me, a young girl who wanted more than was allotted for me in my small town. I knew I had to go get it.

I had no idea what university would be like, but knew it included living in St. John's at a dormitory with students from other parts of the province, Canada and the world. I wanted to go with my whole heart. (And as I have learned, anything you want with your whole heart is bound to happen.)

The university application was the document that would take me to my dreams. I cannot recall a day in my life when I felt more special than I did that day with my few friends, who, like me, were ready to go on to a rich, exciting life. At sixteen, I was still a kid, but I did not see it that way. I was on the verge of freedom, at the doorstep of possibility.

PART I

KNOCKED UP

fog lay
heavy on the water
a kind of night in day
I sauntered
along the shore
wet hair
sticking to my brow
damp woollen coat
hands pushed deep
in pockets
a solitary figure
lost in shivering grey
seeking some quiet
space to think
feet on the beach
grey rocks scratching
beneath my heels
the sound
the feel
unvaried step after step
suddenly
out of the fog
a yellow dory
pulled up on the land wash
her bright yellow
drew me in
beckoning rest
I lay down inside
closed my eyes

*drifting on
imagined waves
lulled into
a tranquil sleep
to dream
my tragic self
let down a river
like Lady of Shalott
who forgot herself
for love*

academic

I felt entirely out of place when I arrived at Memorial, and yet completely in my element once I joined the English department. The kids from St. John's had attended far better schools than me, schools where they could take physics and biology rather than having to choose between them. Where teachers did not advise girls to take biology because physics would be too great a challenge (implied: for their small, delicate brains), where your math teacher would not tell you that he saw you as a future secretary or, if you were lucky, even a teacher. I would show him. I did not need luck.

Walking into the English department was like arriving home. I knew in my bones that I belonged there. But these kids had travelled Europe. They were worldly and educated. They had seen Oxford, the Thames and Buckingham Palace. They had visited Notre Dame. They spoke French with ease and knew Latin. They could name artists by looking at their paintings; the great composers were the background music to their lives. They had studied Shakespeare in high school and could recite sonnets from memory. They were the version of me I had dreamed I could be and wished to be, even more so once I was among them.

I assumed it was obvious that I was a girl from around the bay. God, how could it not be obvious? But I loved being at university anyway. The library was my mecca. Rows and rows of books. The smell and touch of them made me giddy. Never had I seen so many books, so full of ideas and possibilities. My library card was the magic connection between me and all that those books held for me. I would sit among the stacks, pull a book at random and just start reading. I stepped into the pages, a literary visitor of sorts. I lugged armfuls back to my room, so I could have them close and read them into the night as the rest of the dorm slept. The magic wand of knowledge waved over me.

I tried not to care about what I lacked, to read my way to belonging. I would become the girl who had lived inside my imagination almost since I was born, the one who knew that words were my calling.

Christmas 1982

At the end of exams in December 1982, I headed home for Christmas. It was a typical, bitter and snowy Newfoundland winter, where the icy air driven in from the North Atlantic could stop your breath and chill you to the bone. As I did each time I travelled from university to home, I took a taxi, a large van that transported at least ten of us from St. John's to my hometown.

The driver arrived in St. John's from the Burin Peninsula at midday or later, started the home trip about 3:00 p.m., and had to traverse the city to pick up each passenger before we could set out on the highway. I had the misfortune of being picked up early and was on board for the roundabout pickups, a part of the journey I didn't enjoy. The sole advantage was the best choice of seats, and I preferred to sit directly behind the driver, a window to my left and only one person beside me in the row.

On that December day, there was only a short time to read and pass the time. The sky was cloudy with shades of evening settling in. Once it was dark and I could read no more, I had to endure incessant Christmas music on VOCM radio along with the prattle of the passengers, whose thick "bay-men" accents did little to make them more interesting to me. It seemed everyone knew everyone, and I studiously kept to myself, my youth still a good excuse for rudeness.

Once out on the highway, I tried to sleep until we made it to the town of Goobies, where the driver pulled in so people could go into the restaurant attached to the gas station for supper. It was the half-way point of the drive, where the Trans-Canada Highway intersected with the Burin Peninsula Highway. I never ate, so it was just another hour to be endured before the trip resumed, but the other passengers eagerly exited the bus, lumbering in to find a seat in the restaurant in their heavy winter coats and snow boots. Big orders of fish and chips or chicken dinners with heaps of mashed potatoes and gravy were standard fare, prepared by a large and hearty local woman whose cooking was deemed "almost as good as Mom's." Tasty food and lots of it. Her homemade bread was sold on the stands in the adjacent gas station. "Some good, my dear," was often remarked about her cooking and especially the hefty loaves of white bread with golden crusts. To me, though, no one even came close to my mother's cooking and home-made bread, no matter how good.

I visited the restroom, taking my time to conduct my business and check my hair. After that, I wandered through the gas station, browsing magazines and selecting a chocolate treat to tide me over for the remainder of the ride. Then I made my way back to the taxi to sit in the cool and quiet by myself. Through the restaurant window, I could see the other passengers talking and eating, most of them with their coats still on. Average, honest people who took a taxi because they would never think of driving in St. John's. A day or so in the city sent them rushing home with relief. I knew this because, on every trip that I made, it was invariably spoken of with the driver as we made our way back to the Burin Peninsula. "Yes bye, some good to get out of St. John's. Can't wait to get back home now. Shockin' lot of traffic in there. Makes me head giddy." The driver would nod in agreement and reply, "Yes, my son. No place like home. I likes to get in and out of St. John's as quick as I can. Yis, sir."

When the meal was done, I watched the other passengers line up at the till. Everyone paid in cash, counting out the right amount in excruciating exactitude. Then they trooped off to the restrooms before rejoining me in the taxi. The taxi driver came out to stand at the corner of the bus, smoking a cigarette as he shifted from foot to foot, stamping on the snow and ice to stay warm. He made sure he had everyone on board before he took one last puff, flicked his cigarette butt into the snow and climbed back into his seat. Rubbing his hands to warm them, he'd call out, "Everybody on board?" Someone responded, "I spose bye. If not, what odds. Let 'em walk home from here." Then everyone snickered as we pulled back onto the Trans-Canada and made the left turn onto the Burin Peninsula highway.

Once in Marystown, generally sometime past 8:00 p.m., the driver began delivering passengers to their addresses. Front-door service. I arrived in my parent's driveway thankful to see the familiar lights of home and my mother peeking out the window, the curtain lifted at the corner. Excited, she stepped out into the frosty air to greet me with warm hugs. She was glad I was safely home. I knew she would have been leaning from her work in the kitchen to see out the window whenever a car passed up the road, hoping with each new set of lights that the vehicle would turn in the driveway to deliver me. She rushed me inside, where homemade soup and bread were waiting. In that moment the trip fell away, the many hours on the road worth it to be home once more.

My mother made soup on days that I travelled home. She wanted to be sure there was a hot meal ready, whatever time I arrived. My mom and dad gathered at the table with me to talk about how the drive had been, the conditions of the road, and any funny stories I had to relate. One trip, there had been a drunken fool who sang and cursed the whole way. I was appalled that he had been allowed to travel like that, but the driver may have felt a moral obligation to deliver him home to his family. My dad knew the guy I spoke of and had his own stories to relate about the scalawag. The warmth of the kitchen, my mom's soup and the laughter and closeness of my parents were the first and best gifts of my Christmas holiday.

My mother loved nothing more than having her kids around her at Christmas. She knew that I would help decorate the house and tree. I generally spent a day rearranging the living room furniture, deciding where the tree should go, fiddling with the decorating until I was finally satisfied. I reconfigured and moved furniture to other rooms, redesigning the living room so that the Christmas tree was our focal point. She never complained when I recreated her space. She would say, "Do whatever you like. I will put it all back the way I want it when Christmas is over." Then she would make for the kitchen to resume her baking, singing hymns and Christmas carols as she went about it.

On Christmas Eve, our extended family gathered at our house after church to sing carols and enjoy festive punch along with finger foods and Christmas cookies. Getting that organized was my forte, and again my mother left me to it. I worked hard to make Christmas special at our home. It gave me pleasure to prepare food that would impress, and I was known in my family for adding my own touch to things. I tried each year to come up with something new and interesting, such as the year I discovered cheese balls covered in nuts and surrounded by crackers. My brothers teased me for being different. I didn't care. Their teasing was a part of being home.

I enjoyed the anticipation of Christmas much more than the actual day itself. There was something about wrapped presents under the twinkling tree lights and all of us together that made love and connection more tangible. I never wanted those Christmas Eves to end. My oldest brother played his guitar and sang with us, sometimes past midnight. He would wink across the room at me, and I swear my heart could have burst, I felt so happy looking at him. I have maintained a lifelong love of singing carols, as they instantly take me home to those Christmas Eves and my family. When my brother finally put his guitar back in its case and the music was over, we sent everyone out into the winter night with joyful wishes of Merry Christmas, the sound of our laughter ringing into the frozen air.

My mother made sure there were flannel sheets on my bed because she knew I delighted in their coziness. Snuggling into them in the silence that night in 1982, I thought of how good it was to have a family like mine. There are not many presents that I can recall distinctly, but the happiness we shared was the gift I treasured most each year. I did not know it was to be my last Christmas as a carefree young girl, that I would never again come home with the open heart I had that year.

Hurrying to get ready to go home for Christmas, I had neglected a crucial task. My birth control prescription was at an end, and a visit to my doctor was required to renew it. I told myself that I could do it in Marystown, but I knew that would not happen. I would not have been able to tell my mother I was going to the doctor and did not want to chance a male doctor looking at me scornfully. Worse, I did not want someone telling my mother they had seen me at the drugstore buying birth control.

I finally convinced myself that it would be fine—I would make an appointment with my doctor as soon as I got back to St. John's. A few days would not matter. Surely, no one got pregnant for having missed a week or so of birth control pills. I was about to enter the last semester of my bachelor's degree and was on track to graduate and go onto my master's.

With all I had planned and the success I had earned, the idea I might get pregnant seemed foolish.

Well, "how foolish" was right.

something good
from
something bad
can be had
make you
stronger
after a
long time
of
making sense
of why
it happened
to you
at all

bad boy

If it is possible to know the exact moment of conception, I remember it distinctly. I returned to St. John's anxious to see my boyfriend after our separation over Christmas. I telephoned as soon as I made it to my apartment, and he came right over. My roommate was still in Toronto, so we had the place to ourselves. We were happy to be together again and spent the afternoon talking, making dinner and catching up. Then, of course, we fell into intimacy. No inclination to think or stop. We lay afterwards in a tangle of arms and legs, smiling and relaxed. Something was different. I cannot say what it felt like exactly, but that moment has remained with me ever since as the one in which my eldest son was created. In love—young, sweet, naïve love.

My boyfriend and I had a charming, typical-of-university romance. (I'll call him Rob because it's nothing at all like his name.) We met in the single political science course I took. Sitting in the first class, I was focused on the introductory remarks of the impressive female professor when Rob walked in. Late. He was well-dressed and carried his books by his hips with a swagger that seemed deliberate. His hair was swept back from his face, revealing dramatic blue eyes. He looked around in obvious anticipation of being noticed. Instantly, I could see that he was popular, self-assured and on the hunt for opportunity.

He smiled expectantly at the professor. She frowned with annoyance and carried on. She made it clear she did not appreciate being interrupted once her class was in session, and I felt the same. Rob sat in the row next to me, one seat behind, and I did my best to ignore him.

There was an awkward tap on my shoulder. I turned and found myself looking right into those bright eyes. He leaned closer and whispered, "Can you pass me the handouts?" as he motioned to the stack on the empty desk in front of me. I gave him my best pompous smirk and whispered, "If you want handouts, you should make it to class on time like the rest of us." Then I turned back to the professor, knowing full well he was sitting there with a shocked look and an open mouth. I was delighted I had unnerved him, perhaps getting his attention at the same time.

At the end of class, he followed me into the hallway and again reached out to tap me on the shoulder. He looked me up and down with interest as he said, "Excuse me—would you like to get a cup of coffee with me?" This boy was something, all right. I replied, "I don't drink coffee," and then walked away from him, not looking back. I felt him watching, and a secretive smile crept across my lips. I was already looking forward to the next class.

He chased me out of class several times in the following weeks, before, in exasperation, he finally asked what it would take to get to see me. Surprised, intrigued and aware that I could only hold out for so long before he lost interest, I offered, "If you really want to see me, I am in the library in the evenings. If you care to join me to study, you can see me there." I fully expected it would be the end of his pursuit. I figured that, after coffee, his most likely date suggestion would be a nightclub, drinking and dancing in the hope of sex at the evening's end.

I misjudged him.

That evening I was in the periodicals room with my books spread out in front of me on a wide wooden table, deep in research and thought. I heard him before I saw him. As I looked up, he excused himself to a group of students he was making his way through as he searched the room. He spotted me, waved and came over to take a seat across from me. Openly pleased with himself for having found me, he smiled and whispered, "What do we do now?" Unable to repress a pleased smile myself, I said, "Now we study." And we did. We frequently stole glances across the table, but we mostly worked. When the library lights dimmed to signal it was ten minutes to closing, we gathered up our books and strolled down the stairs and out the main entrance. We walked through the darkened campus and began a relationship that lasted more than thirteen years.

We were pretty much inseparable from then on. He came to the arts building where most of my classes were just to ride with me in the elevator up to my floor, kissing me passionately as soon as the doors closed. Sometimes we stayed on the elevator to go up and down several times, giggling if the doors opened, revealing us to those stepping on. I was late for class a couple of times, telling him afterwards that he was a bad influence. I had now become the one annoying the professor. He laughed and told me it was worth it.

On several Friday evenings, he accompanied me to campus productions of Shakespeare. He leaned in close to me so that I could explain characters, plot and language, and to kiss my cheek. He held my hand and mischievously touched my inner thigh so that I blushed and playfully tugged away. Shakespeare was the backdrop to our blossoming romance. I liked that Rob made an effort to appreciate my interests and I especially liked having him next to me in a darkened theatre where we could hold hands. He had grown up in a family that valued the arts, literature and music, and his interest in them pleased me. My past boyfriends had lacked sorely in intellectual conversation. Few were readers, and the only music they listened to was rock 'n' roll. I had gone for looks over brains, so it was compelling to meet a boy with both.

Rob loved cars, particularly German cars. In our university days, he had several Volkswagen Beetles that were always in various states of disrepair. The heaters in them never worked, so we had to be careful not to breathe towards the windshield to prevent a buildup of frost and ice in winter. One had gaping holes in the floor, which meant that every time we went over muddy potholes, I had to lift my feet to avoid getting soaked. And there are a lot of potholes in Newfoundland! When we drove to visit my family in Marystown, he wrapped me in a sleeping bag so I wouldn't freeze. I looked like a mummy strapped in beside him, but I was warm and amused by our off-beat adventure.

We joked about the foibles of those cars, which gave each one an endearing personality. We spent many a Saturday driving to a small town just outside St. John's to visit Rob's favourite German car expert and repair guy. It was his genuine friendliness and kindness towards people like the old German that revealed his goodness. Rob was born into an affluent family, but he was an everyman's man. I often thought he was most comfortable and at ease with ordinary people.

Rob took to my family readily. The first time he came to visit and stay with me at my parent's house, I paced from window to window, watching for him to pull up in the latest Beetle. I worried that he would think my parents unsophisticated and plain. My dad was outside doing yard work—I did not dare ask him to stop and come inside, but I wished that he would. I did not want Rob's first impression to be Dad's yard overalls and rubber boots. I loved my dad immensely and wanted to protect him from judgement. I also did not want to be embarrassed by our small-town ways, where dads did their own yard work and wore work clothes to do it. My father was oblivious, and even if he had been aware of me pacing and fretting, he would have laughed and carried on. My father was not one to compromise his ways for anyone, something that took me some time to properly appreciate.

I wanted Rob to see Dad as the man he was—a funny, witty, smart storyteller who was kind and generous to all. Watching from the window that day, I thought my dad looked like a labourer that Rob's parents might hire. Rob's father was a heavily credentialed doctor who drove a BMW that he had travelled to Germany to handpick. My dad drove a Chevy pick-up that he paid cash for at a local dealer. They were worlds apart.

What I did not see then was that there are values much more important than credentials, wealth and accolades. My dad was solid. He was honest and forthright. He was a good man, an honourable husband, whose position in life was everything that he wanted it to be. He was the best father. The kind of dad who, when he approached the end of his life, told me that the only thing that really matters is love. "Love," he said, "is the best of what we have while we are here; it's the only thing we take with us, and also leave behind, when we die." His was wisdom and understanding derived from a life well lived. But in my youthful desperation to impress a boy, I would have preferred my dad be inside wearing a shirt and tie as he read the paper. That fantasy was not about to happen.

My mother was in the kitchen preparing food and worrying over what to feed Rob. She had asked me several times what he liked, and I reassured her that he would eat anything. I did not know if that was true, but I was too stressed about his being in our small house to care about the details of his culinary preferences. Rob lived in a spacious Victorian home in the most desirable neighbourhood in St. John's; his bedroom had its own fireplace and built-in cupboards with individual compartments for hats, with hat boxes inside them. There were fifteen-foot ceilings throughout, inlaid hardwood floors and a vast, gorgeous stained-glass window that framed and lit the circular staircase. The modest bungalow my dad had built with his own hands was considered "nice" in our small town, but after living in the city, I realized it lacked the grandeur I now wished it could magically assume.

Then the little blue Volkswagen pulled in. My dad was right in the centre of the lawn with his garden rake, and Rob climbed sprightly out of his car and strode over to shake my dad's hand and introduce himself. I knew that would impress my dad—he appreciated my friends who took the time to be personable. They stood talking for a few minutes while I looked on from behind the bedroom window curtain. I could not hear what they were saying, but the tilt of my dad's head and the occasional laughter let me breathe again. Eventually, my dad motioned for him to go on inside, and I jumped from my hiding spot to greet him and introduce him to my mother. She was waiting in the kitchen with her apron tied around her waist and a counter full of her morning's baking.

As we gathered for supper at the kitchen table, Rob made a great fuss over the food my mother had prepared. He ate and talked and seemed to truly enjoy being with my parents and my kid sister. From time to time, he looked at me and winked. My parents seemed relaxed and normal, and I was finally able to relax as well. Later, when we were alone, I confessed that I'd been apprehensive about him meeting my family and seeing where I lived. He put his arms around me and said it was all perfect. I knew it was a world far removed from his own, but he embraced it with ease. In those days, and in those ways, I loved him.

I was the smart girl who he had finally convinced to date him. He said that, until me, no girl had refused him. Doing so had spurred his relentless pursuit. We did not fall madly in love; we didn't even start out aiming to be long term. He had been quite clear with me that it was a "thing" that we would move on from eventually and I agreed and went along with that plan. He was the one who changed it up.

The day came when he said he wanted to have a serious conversation with me, and I assumed he would break off our relationship. Instead, he said that he wanted us to be exclusive. Surprising myself, I was eager. It may have been then that he told me he loved me and, while we didn't say "I love you" frequently, I knew it was there. I had scored the most popular guy in St. John's and girls openly told me of their interest in him, but I was more pleased about what we shared.

Yet there was a lot we didn't share. In his circle of friends, there were wealthy girls with sexy, fashionable clothes, shoes and hairstyles.

My money went to tuition, books, housing and food, with little left over. I would stand at my closet surveying my paltry wardrobe, hoping for inspiration to hit and make something out of the nothing I saw in there. Going out on a date left me longing for an outfit I would be proud to wear in front of the girls I caught looking me over with un-apologetic disdain, the ones with the cars, means and attitudes of the privileged. I was a bay girl, my hair a mess of curls that would not be tamed into anything resembling sophisticated.

One evening, as Rob sprawled on my bed waiting for me to get dressed, I told him my dilemma. We were heading to a house party where I would be up close and personal with the worst of the girls I dreaded. He was amused. Finally, nearing exasperation, I said, "Well, if they look at me critically, and of course they will, I will ask who among them would like to discuss King Lear's descent into madness?" He burst out laughing and encouraged me, "by all means," to put them in their non-intellectual place. I laughed too. I decided that night to go as my-self and forget my fashion shortcomings. I knew they were jealous that I had scooped the boy who was, by any measure, the most popular and desired. When he looked at me across a room, I felt beautiful and smart.

He was the bad boy of my young dreams.

From that first night in the library, he continued to study with me. When he graduated, his parents told me privately that they had never expected him to earn a degree and gave me credit for having helped him achieve it. I told them that he did the work and deserved the cred-it, but I was pleased to be recognized as a positive influence. Together, we enjoyed university. During the week, we went to our classes and studied. On weekends, we went to parties and danced until the band stopped playing.

Rob was my first love story. Not a deep or abiding love, but that first foray into romance and sexual partnership. We were busy having fun and growing up at the same time, and he was everything I wanted. Irreverent, daring, sexy, surprising. I gave myself over to him and never looked back. In my eyes, he was the best blend of bad and excitement. In those early days, I could not have imagined where we were headed or how it would end.

As the signs of change crept in, I tried to ignore them. In our last semester, he revealed a cruel streak, his tongue becoming critical and his actions harsh.

I was pregnant. While neither of us spoke about it or admitted it, it was present between us. He was preoccupied with finding a job after graduation and buying his first new car and a motorcycle. Shortly after graduation, he had all three. He was establishing himself and entering the adult world. I was silently struggling with what I knew we had to face, afraid he would leave me.

One night, as we drove on the crosstown parkway in his new Volkswagen Rabbit, an argument erupted. We shouted at each other. Our arguments were becoming more frequent. Meaner. In the middle of shouting, he reached across the seat and hit me so hard that my head bounced off the window. We instantly fell silent. I was stunned. I stared ahead, blinking through my tears as he drove on, faster and faster. He told me that night that I needed to listen to him. The message was that it was my fault that he had hit me.

I might have left him. I should have left him. I should have called him on it. But I was pregnant and scared. My life was coming apart in a way I did not have the nerve to handle alone.

The next time he hit me, it was in my stomach. I wondered if he was hitting me there because he was angry with what he knew was happening inside me. Neither of us could undo it.

I hated him bitterly for hitting me and, while in time I learned to forgive him, I have never forgotten what it did to me. It's an ugly place, being trapped and ruled by anger. I am not proud that I stayed, but I have forgiven myself for lacking the strength to leave. In retrospect, we were both broken. I came to accept that Rob fought his own demons, regrets and loss. What he did was unacceptable, but it was influenced by those we loved, by society and by things left unsaid between us.

I used to go back over that Christmas of 1982 and wish, hopelessly, that I could do it over. I would get the birth control pills before I went home. Or I would force myself to go to the doctor in Marystown, with a big "screw you" to nosey neighbours. Or I would tell Rob, that day of my return, how my birth control prescription had run out and that we needed a condom. As I daydreamed about each of those scenarios, I felt a momentary sense of relief for making a better choice. Then, after going through each one, I would sit back and sigh, knowing that nothing could undo what had happened. I took the risk that women are warned not to take when using birth control. I had unprotected sex. I jumped into it not thinking or caring, overtaken by desire that outranked logic.

*I will
take an adventure
all my own
away from home
and what I know*

*to see
who I am
and
what I can
be
as me*

January 1983

The bells of that New Year's Eve rang in my year of change. I was in the final semester of my bachelor's degree; I had worked diligently and was proud of my accomplishments. I was accepted into the English Honours program. I had come a long way from my humble community school and had entered a scholarly academia to which I felt ideally suited. This last semester was to be the best and most important of my undergraduate achievements.

The honours program required an additional year beyond the normal four-year degree requirements. That year included the prescribed honours course and covered English literature from early Anglo-Saxon times to modern day. The objective was the required A grade on a comprehensive exam at the end of the final semester, preparation for which took considerable effort on top of my regular course load. I had mostly As to that point and intended to ace the exam and each of my courses in the final semester. A master of arts and then a PhD in English were in sight. The idea that I would become "Dr. Hodder" had become tangible, believable—even for me.

In the English department, there was a female professor who had the most beautifully appointed office I had ever seen. In the middle was an elegant cherrywood desk with curved, carved legs and a large living-room-style lamp. Behind the desk, she sat in a floral print wing-back chair, a signature of comfort and grace. Much of the floor was covered with a deep red Persian rug. The art on the walls revealed the culture and taste of a well-travelled woman. On a side table sat a tea set with a silver teapot and floral china cups and saucers. Her office had a storybook quality and captivated my eyes as well as my imagination. Especially on dark winter afternoons, I lingered for as long as I could without being noticed when I passed her office, stopping to admire the warm, inviting atmosphere while the professor sipped tea and worked in her lovely surroundings. As classical music drifted softly out the door, I decided an office like hers would be mine someday. I saw myself greeting students and discussing literature and poetry while my surroundings spoke of my appreciation of finer things, my travels and my knowledge of art and eminent writers. It was not just a daydream—it was an irrepressible vision of who I was becoming.

By February, though, I was consumed with a very different vision. I had missed my period twice, and the tender swelling in my breasts could not be ignored. Yet, I tried to ignore it. I decided I was overreacting; my period would reappear. I put it down to the stress of the final semester and the pressure I was under to perform well. What I envisioned for my life could not include pregnancy or a child. Such things did not happen to the kind of woman who sat in a beautiful office where Mozart was the soundtrack to thoughtful ponderings. That woman was composed, intelligent and poised for greatness. She was elegant and highly regarded by those around her. She was not the girl who got pregnant. She was not the girl who messed things up by being careless. But she was also not me.

As the reality of my pregnancy slowly set in, I felt more and more off balance. I was the girl who had left small-town ways and housewife servitude for an academic, intellectual, independent life. I had been smug enough to think I was better than those I left behind.

It had only taken one swift indiscretion to bring me down. Not only was I no better than those unfortunate girls in high school, my attitude toward them at the time probably made me worse. I was older and had access to birth control. I lived on a university campus where I could walk into the clinic between classes and get a birth control prescription. I had no excuse for getting pregnant.

When I think about how afraid I was that my mother would find out I was having sex, it seems absurd now. She knew I had a boyfriend. I lived on my own. Of course I was having sex. But in those days, when you brought your boyfriend home, you slept in separate beds, in different rooms. She believed that the worst thing that could happen to a girl was to get pregnant before she was married.

In my case, she was right.

I crawled inside my disappointment in myself and spent my last semester hoping and pleading for a miracle. It took considerable effort to pretend everything was normal. I lost weight and grew pale. I told no one. I got up every day and trudged through the snow to campus, carrying a growing fetus inside me. I studied, attended class, ate and tried to live as though nothing was wrong. I even somehow managed to achieve my academic goals. On the day of the comprehensive exam, I read each of the literary passages that I had to identify for the author, literary title, period of publication, context and meaning. I don't know how I knew them all, but I did. I had been worried that I would draw a blank and lose my honours degree, but I found out within a day of writing the exam that I had been successful. On that front, at least, I was safe.

I've been told I was strong to have managed to live through that last semester and get good grades, but I'm not convinced it was strength. I felt mostly fear, waiting for someone to mock me the way I had cruelly mocked those girls in high school. I pushed the reality of my situation down inside me, determined to deal with it later while holding onto a futile hope that it would somehow cease to be true.

When the day came to buy a dress for my graduation ceremony, I had to choose one that fit loosely around my growing middle. I sat for graduation photos at a studio, smiling meekly into a camera that seemed to search my face for what was inside me. I hated those photos. Looking at them, I saw a frightened girl who could not smile. I walked the stage on graduation day feeling flushed inside my robes, fearful that when the chancellor placed my English Honours hood over my head and shoulders, I might slip off the kneeling stool, fainting onto the floor in front of everyone. It was the moment I had worked for and deserved, but the last place in the world I wanted to be that day was on a stage in front of a crowded audience.

My degree remains in the burgundy and gold-embossed folder presented to me on graduation day. I have never taken it out or made any effort to buy a frame and put it on a wall. It is somewhere in a box, stored away. Later, I gave up the full fellowship that I was awarded for my master's degree. I never pursued it. I never became the professor with the elegant office where students came to discuss the literary greats. No pleasurable hours debating the power of poetry to light your soul.

Why not, you may ask.

That dream died in me. I lost my will. I lost my belief that I had ever been good enough—because in the months after, I failed myself and a child in the worst way imaginable.

For years, I set my love of writing aside. After all, what could I write except the truth? A truth that swallowed the hopeful girl. I made my way, a different way, but there have been many times I regretted having left my academic life. I see now that my story may have made me a more interesting professor. The one who might have inspired her students to love literature and poetry as a means of coping with struggles, with life's turns and revelations. I might have made my office a refuge and a safe place. I was the stories and poems I read, and the plays I watched, but I could not see past my failures and my self-imposed sentence. Instead of allowing others to reject me, I rejected myself on their behalf and without their consent. It made sense at the time.

I have had many offices over the years. I decorated each one to create the kind of peacefulness and beauty that I saw in my professor's office. I worked in higher education for over twenty years and met with countless students and staff in my offices. My leadership focused on my mission to help others. I asked questions to uncover who people are and to understand their motivation and longings in life. I encouraged them to live their dreams. I helped them tell their stories, knowing that in those stories were maps of their desires and their pain as well as their ways to triumph. It is who I became—through the map of my own story.

*I am
the wrong end
of the story
the outcome
and the at last
of what was done
in the past
there's no going back
to change it
or reclaim it
so here I sit
with regret
in the pit
of my stomach
an ache
that won't go
or slow
with time*

bathroom Jesus

In the winter of 1983, there were nights I sat on the toilet so long the imprint of its seat became a vivid red welt on my butt and thighs. In the top of the old Victorian house where I had my apartment on Circular Road in St. John's, the small bathroom had a slanted ceiling so low that I could reach up and touch it as I sat. I pushed on the ceiling and strained, praying for that drop of red to appear in the toilet. I called out to Jesus. Not in a religious, praise God, hallelujah kind of way. It was more a dark, desperate, I will give you my soul if you save me sort of plea.

I talked to Jesus, implored him, negotiated with him. If he would just let my period come, I would change. I vowed to be a better person. I would never have sex again. Or not as much. And always with birth control or a condom. I would do anything. I would serve the poor. I would go back to church to please my mother. I would stop swearing. I promised and strained until sweat ran between my breasts, soaking the front of my shirt. A twenty-one-year-old girl not wanting to accept that she was pregnant, imploring Jesus to intervene and save her sorry ass. It was worth a try. It was all I had.

During those bathroom sessions, I would pee several times, small tinkles in the toilet. I tried not to peek, believing that patience, belief and vision were required. I would close my eyes and visualize a stream of red, concentrating until my head ached. I would eventually dare to look down at the now yellowish water and try to convince myself that there was at least a shade of red in there, sure that if I looked hard enough and long enough it would materialize.

It was pointless and exhausting. After several rounds, when I could no longer take it, I would wipe myself, and with one final, despairing hope I would look at the tissue trying to see even a slight shade of pink. No. Again.

What was all that shit that people said about having prayers answered? I was certain they said if you believe and pray with your whole heart your prayers get answered. Was it the bathroom that was getting in the way? Was Jesus offended by my location and lack of underwear? Were prayers only answered in church? Or if I kneeled beside my bed as my mother had taught me to do when I was a kid? Where was the guidebook to successful prayer? Did the Bible have a section on that? Because, apparently, I missed it.

Dejected, I told myself that the next night Jesus would find time to listen and accept my deal of repentance. I felt certain he would understand that the little bathroom was the only place I had privacy and was also where I needed to confirm, via the toilet, that my period was back. I wanted a direct result. Pray. Bleed. We're done. No more bathroom chats after that. I could relocate to a better, more appropriate venue. I would show up in church and kneel in total blissful grace before the Holy Trinity.

Meanwhile, I pushed the word pregnant out of my mind. I had heard that stress could delay periods. I tried to relax. Of course, I knew the difference. A girl did not miss two periods. I never had. I had been as regular as rain, as the saying goes, since I was thirteen.

The tightness and swelling in my small breasts became more pronounced. I woke at night if I accidentally bumped one in my sleep. If someone hugged me, I had to draw in my breath to stand the discomfort. My bras became uncomfortable. The taut, round boobs I'd longed for in high school (begging my mom for twenty dollars for the miracle creams advertised in teen magazines) had now appeared.

Standing up, clothes back in place, I faced myself in the small mirror above the pedestal sink. Red cheeks and sweat were the only visible outcomes of my strenuous effort. Even my ears were red. In that mirror, I saw my face. Scared. Puffy. Streaked with tears. Jesus, I looked awful. The curls around my forehead were wet with perspiration, and my head throbbed. I was shaky.

I leaned forward and stared into the mirror, trying to see how the girl looking out at me could be me. Her brown eyes still looked like mine, but their brightness had faded. I pulled up my sweaty shirt to examine my stomach. There was no evidence that anything was happening beneath the surface. My waist was still slender and curved. I wondered how long it would take before the bulge would appear and my waist disappear.

The girl in the mirror was me, but not me. A stranger who looked like me, wrought with fear. She was the new me that tried to make deals with Jesus in a bathroom, for crying out loud! Righteous people, I knew, didn't just pray when the going got tough. They prayed all the time and thanked God and Jesus for making their lives so wonderful and perfect and free from sin. They prayed in advance, preventing the sin show that was mine. Showing up with a major problem caused by bodily transgression was not a strong position from which to start a prayer regimen.

I didn't like this new me. I wanted to slap her face and tell her to fuck off. I wanted her to get the hell out of my body. I wanted her to take her nasty business out of my reality. She was screwing with my persona as scholar and soon-to-be graduate. She was making a liar out of me, the girl who said such a thing would never happen to her. Yet there she was in the mirror staring back at me. "Hah! Knocked up! Soon everyone will know what kind of girl you really are," she seemed to say.

Weird as it may sound, I believe Jesus was present in the bathroom with me on those nights. He was there patiently waiting for me to accept my circumstances and get on with a different prayer. A prayer for strength to get me through my last semester, graduation, and the birth of a child before the snow would fly again next fall. I imagined an earthy kind of Jesus, wearing a hemp shirt, dreadlocks and sandals, slightly bored and yawning as he sat off in the corner of the bathroom with his legs crossed, leaning his chin on the palm of his hand, rolling his eyes as I begged for his help. I could imagine him eventually throwing his hands up in the air as I asked him repeatedly, "Please, please, puhleeeezzzzeeeee don't let me be pregnant. I will do anything."

And with that, he would furrow his brow and respond, "Are you done? It's too late." With that, he would yawn, turn away and fade out of the room.

In my mind, that bathroom remains a sort of strange sanctum

where I attempted to connect with the divine. Jesus appeared, not as the long-haired, serene, kind-faced man in the biblical images of my youth, but as a rascally, hard-hitting badass who refused to listen. He was Jesus with an attitude. No forgiveness. No answered prayer. Just raw, brutal honesty. His message? "You chose this. Time to 'fess up and face the consequences."

I was looking for a way out of my problems when what I needed was a way into a place of acceptance. I talked to Jesus as a way to cope rather than as an act of faith. After the many years that have since passed, bathroom Jesus seems kinder, less rascally. Not such a badass after all—more of a realist. He heard my prayers. He listened. He just had a different answer for me. Years later, when I lived in Phoenix, Arizona, I came upon a sign advertising "Jesus' Autobody Repair." I laughed out loud, thinking I might have had better luck getting the answer I wanted if I had been able to pray in that shop. I had, in fact, been seeking my own kind of auto-body repair.

Eventually, I gave up my nightly bathroom quests. I faced my situation with reluctant resolve. On those winter nights, in my poorly insulated apartment, I hid under my heavy bed covers and watched the drapes flutter as the wind whistled in around the corners of the frosted window panes. Warm in my nest, I traced the tiny, emerging curve of my abdomen with my fingertips. Over time it grew pronounced and firm. During those long, dark nights I bore the weight of my secret in silent solitude. I was pregnant. I was not sure how long I could keep it a secret, but for the rest of that winter and into spring it was mine alone.

What I didn't see during those early nights in my pregnancy was the long road ahead. A road with no end.

*I need to stop
comparing me to you
thinking
fuck
you're so much better
your words wiser
I can kill a lot of time
looking at you and
your view of the world
written well
as you tell
stories that confound me
and surround me
with doubt
that I could ever be
that good
I hunker here
alone
breathing life into dreams
resisting the need
to be
like you*

philosophy of life

My English philosophy professor gave me a great gift over the course of the two semesters I spent with him. He was British, pompous and delightfully entangled with the female modern literature professor in the department. The affair was his most beguiling trait, by a long shot. He sashayed down the hallways and ran his fingers through his thinning grey hair with studied distraction. Lean and lanky, he had a strong curved jaw and steely blue eyes that suggested he had been a heartbreaker in his younger days. He had a sexy sort of charisma that made plenty of the female students give him a second glance and giggle behind their hands when they spoke about him.

In class, he relished asking challenging questions, the kind that made us squirm in our seats. He expected us to have read and under-stood the assigned essays in the hefty philosophy text that I carried with me constantly, much to the detriment of my lower back. A question launched, he would lean back, tipping his chair onto its hind legs, to consider your response as he pointedly, purposely made you fear his retort. The idea of getting it right consumed me, whatever right was. I hid at the end of the long table where we gathered for his class, hoping he would forget my existence, but he sought me out like a target.

"Miss Hodder. Let's hear your thoughts," he'd command in his lofty English accent.

I would freeze, sure I would disappoint him and embarrass myself.

"The cat got your tongue?" Amused, disdainful.

I'd finally blurt something, the sound of my own voice strange to me in that quiet space with everyone listening.

Then awkward silence.

My professor, studying my face, would latch onto his upper lip and twist it as he took in what I had offered. I stared at the suede patches on the elbows of his tweed jacket, waiting, my heart beating in my ears. And then, with a great inhalation through his nostrils, he righted his chair, leaned forward and offered a critique of my paltry analysis of the philosophy essay I had read in futile fervour the night before. No matter what he said, I was left to wonder what he really meant and if there was any shred of confirmation for my interpretation. He had the sort of intellect and vocabulary that made me anxious to keep up. I would pull myself in, my face burning, my armpits drenched with perspiration, while I avoided eye contact with the other students. I wanted to disappear. Drop down an Alice in Wonderland rabbit hole and run, run away. I could almost hear the other students thinking "bay girl."

These intellectual volleys went on for some time, further intensifying my dread of being called on. I cursed my earlier education for not having prepared me for such discussions. There was so much I did not know. How was I ever going to make up for my underfunded rural education? I thought I would have to read every book in the library stacks to even come close to being clever enough to answer his questions. I needed an immediate sabbatical to study the ancient philosophers before I could confidently sit in my professor's class. The only small comfort I had was that the other students were also intimidated by him and they were far better educated than me. He tore apart their answers too. As we came to know one another better, we took to retreating to the cafeteria after class to commiserate. Surviving this professor, we knew, required group therapy over coffee and all the sweets we could consume.

Finally, one day he turned to me in front of everyone. Well, all six or so of us who made up the English honours group. Then he said something that became an extraordinary gift.

"Miss Hodder." Long pause.

"Why do you doubt yourself being here?" Another long pause.

I wondered if he expected a response. I gave none. I sat, panicked and immobile, trying to swallow the lump in my throat while my heart seemed about to beat its way out of my chest.

He finally went on. "You are not in my class by accident, Miss Hodder. You are here because you deserve a place at the table. Speak your mind. Don't be afraid of it. I am waiting to actually hear from you. I know you've got it in you. I am waiting for you to share what you know with the rest of us. Stop worrying about being wrong and speak."

I took in his words like a long, cool drink I hadn't realized I'd been thirsty for until that moment.

I deserved a place at the table? I belonged?

Up until that moment, I had read and reread the essays, underlining important points and researching everything that did not make sense to me. Which was a lot. I pulled books from the library stacks to find explanations for passage after passage and then walked home when the library closed, still doubting I had adequately understood what I'd read. And when I was asked to speak, intimidation blocked what was in my brain.

My professor pulled me out of my hiding place that day. His intention was not to embarrass me but to express confidence in me. It seemed he thought I had something to say—me, the girl from around the bay.

Something awakened in me: a belief in myself. Throughout that two-semester class, I went from being reluctant and hesitant to willing and determined. I read the philosophy essays with renewed commitment. I studied them with a trusting mind. I asked questions. I probed for more. I let curiosity lead me instead of fear. I got together with fellow students to study, discuss and prepare for class. I gave up my lonely solitude and the fear of being less-than. I learned that curiosity and willingness open doors to knowledge and opportunity.

I also learned from my professor that it may take someone showing up for you before you can show up for yourself in life. My view of him warmed after that. I saw that his tough demeanour was meant to elicit greater things from his students. I earned a B+ in that class. It was the best grade of my degree. It felt like an A because, at the outset, I had fully expected to fail. The grade was only part of the outcome, the less significant one. The greater part was discovering that everything I need is inside me, waiting to be tapped, a wellspring of limitless potential.

*I sit
in a circle
of light
the wild night
beyond
I warm
my small hands
and
my beating heart
in the glow
I know not
if I ought
leave this light
I might
never
find my way
back
and suffer
always
from the lack
of it*

heroes and legends

My final year of university was spent studying and translating, line by line, the epic Anglo-Saxon poem *Beowulf*. One other female student and I took two semesters of Old English together; our professor received special permission from the head of the English department to teach the two of us in his office. Classes normally required a minimum of five students, but no other students would agree to take the advanced class in their last year of the program. Shocking, I know. The others were grateful and relieved to have the requisite Old and Middle English courses safely behind them.

The two of us begged our beloved Anglo-Saxon professor to teach us, and, pleased, he came up with the idea of teaching us in his office. Taking that course with him was my favourite university experience. Under his tutelage, translating *Beowulf* line by line was a treasured accomplishment and a joy. We curled ourselves into big leather chairs as we learned to roll the guttural old English sounds from the back of our throats and off the tip of our tongues. Slowly the Anglo-Saxon lexicon started to sound natural to our ears, and we came to understand words and phrases without translation. If people heard us, they surely wondered what language we were speaking and why we were having so much fun doing it. Each letter in each word had to be enunciated. It made me realize how lazy we English speakers have become as so many letters have gone silent. Speaking Anglo-Saxon was exercise for all parts of the mouth and the diaphragm. While not a pretty language, for the most part, it was moving, expressive and haunting. I was grateful to experience the poem as it was originally meant to be heard.

As winter set in, snow drifted and swirled outside the tall window at the end of the office, while the lamplight within that tiny space warmed us. It was the optimal setting, taking us out of our lives and back into a raw, spirited and dangerous time to learn the epic tale of a hero named Beowulf. I doubt that I would ever have appreciated the story as much as I do had I not studied it in its original language. So much is lost in translation—the feel of the story, the fear and the dread of the monster, Grendel.

My professor's South African accent stays with me, the melodic intonation of his voice along with his excitement as he led our discussions. He was small in stature but impressive in every other way. Underneath his academic robes, he wore impeccable suits and ties, with crisp white shirts that highlighted his meticulously groomed grey beard and mischievous, sparkling blue eyes. He looked at us over the top of clear-framed glasses, a mixture of humour and pleasure on his face. He lit up that little office with his appreciation of *Beowulf,* and his flawless elocution of Anglo-Saxon made me fall in love with the language.

He was the professor who, as he met me in the hall one day, made a comment that I have since cherished. He came striding towards me with aplomb, his robes floating behind him, his head lifted proudly. He put up his hand politely to stop me. "Miss Hodder. Let me offer you a compliment. You walk with such poise and grace. You are very striking. As you become a woman, this will serve you well. Remember that." Then he smiled that smile of his that said he was delighted to have said something of impact and importance and walked on. I watched him go, letting his words sink in. Having grown up a skinny, curly-haired girl in the 1970s when straight, silky blond hair and curves were preferred, I had never had anyone observe me in that way. It was as though he had removed the blinds so that I could see myself as I was meant to be seen, and I was grateful.

In my professor's small office, I was lost in my vision of the bard hall. I imagined the warmth from a huge, open, stone fireplace and the glow of candles, providing the only cheer for those gathered around the mead table. The people in the hall were huddled together, the walls around them their shelter against the wild, dark night. Whatever lay beyond the doors, out on the moorlands, incited fear in their hearts and hope in the one called Beowulf. He was the only one that could guard and save them from Grendel. Beowulf was the only one brave enough, strong enough, skilled enough and fearless enough to fight that monster. With bread and meat on their pewter boards, I imagined them hoisting their mead cups to toast the night and their hero.

I could have fallen for a hero like Beowulf. I would have eagerly lifted my skirts for him, throwing my slender arms about his strong neck as I surrendered my body and my innocence. And when he left, I would have defiantly kissed him in front of everyone, pushing the sweetness of my tongue deep in his mouth, feeling the swell of his desire against me—to be sure he had reason to defeat Grendel and return to my soft caresses. With a man like that, a baby would be the bounty of our love. A blessed son to emulate his father's mighty legacy, or a willful daughter who would strap on a sword in the middle of the night and secretly ride off to join a battle, proving that girls too are mighty warriors.

Beowulf was the kind of rugged man who inspired me to pursue the proverbial bad boy, the kind of man I sought and measured all other men against. Like a steamy, drugstore romance novel. Alas, the man who had planted his seed in me was a bad boy but not a hero, at least not for me.

As honours students, we had our own study room where we assembled to read, discuss, eat or take time out. One afternoon I was nauseous and especially tired. I lay down on the couch and instantly fell asleep, a deep sleep brought on by the powerful changes happening in my body. It was unlike me, but irresistible, and I didn't care where I was or what I looked like.

Sometime later I woke up, blinking slowly back into consciousness. For a moment, I thought my reality was the dream. Pregnant? Just a dream. But then ...

No. Not a dream. My fellow Anglo-Saxon classmate walked in and, seeing me lying there, groggy and listless, asked if I was okay. I lied and said yes. She assumed I was ill, and I was glad to let her think so. She was married to one of the other honours students and was pregnant that last year too. I used to look at her and wonder if pregnancy was something you could smell on another person if you were pregnant yourself. She was buoyantly pregnant, fully in the blush of the happy mother-to-be. She delighted in her belly with unhurried emphasis as she stroked its round circumference with loving, motherly hands. She talked about her bodily changes to the extent that it was awkward for the rest of us and unbearable for me.

She also had the unnerving trait of openly staring at people. I once caught her staring at me, and I was sure she was about to blurt out, "You're pregnant." It did not come out of her mouth, but I still think she may have known. She frequently studied me in an off-handed way as we settled ourselves into our professor's office for class. On one occasion she even said, "I can't help looking at people with flat bellies now that mine has grown so large." I was still small enough to fit inside my jeans even as the zipper and button strained for closure. Yet, having her constantly staring at me was discomfiting. I worried she was sniffing out my secret.

She wore practical shoes and Irish cable-knit sweaters and her long, straight red hair was only ever styled into braids, at most. Her baby would be breastfed and later fed only foods my friend made herself. Cloth diapers, nothing plastic or paper. No television. She played Mozart and Beethoven and read Shakespeare to the baby still in her womb. She was the wholesome earth mother, beautifully content in her rosy roundness. I tried to dislike her, but she was so earnest and lovely that I could not resist adoring her. (She had also agreed to take advanced Anglo-Saxon with me, a winning attribute.) Still, she made me more aware of my dilemma at times when I needed to focus on Beowulf; keeping my secret was stressful. Where I might have had her care and support, I chose fear. Isolation. I led a double life, that of a scholar and that of a secret-keeper. I was one of the honours students, and I was dishonoured, at least in my mind. I have learned that you can be a lot of things inside yourself and that you can fool others most of the time. But the day comes when you must become your truth. If I could revisit my old friend, I would tell her that her presence has remained with me as an example of what it means to be authentic. I did not see it then, but it is clear to me now that she was a young woman blossoming into her beautiful circumstances. Had I confided in her, I believe she would have welcomed me into her concern and care. Oh, but for the courage to have chosen another way.

At the end of the year, my professor gave me an inscribed copy of his personal, published translation of *Beowulf* as a graduation gift. I have often looked at that book to remember who I was. Who I might have become. The girl who came to university despite the odds against her, and finally felt that she belonged there—who proved to herself that she was smart and worthy enough to be at the table and in the conversation. The girl who walked with poise and grace.

The girl who completed her degree while guarding a secret.

button up your coat
she said
it's cold outside
take your mittens
here's your hat
and don't forget your lunch
off you go
to school
don't forget the golden rule
hurry now
don't be late
I'll be right here waiting
when the day is done
and you come
running
through the door

~ my mother

graduation

My parents and younger sister came to St. John's to celebrate my graduation at the end of May. As was common in Newfoundland, my family stayed with me in my small apartment, partly to save money and partly because being with family was a priority. It was seldom that my family stayed in a hotel, although, on this occasion, I wished they would. As soon as they arrived, my mother was in the kitchen preparing food and making sure we all had plenty to eat. She brought pies and cookies and, my favourite, homemade bread from home. She had a way of taking over the kitchen and was most pleased when she was in charge. She made it look easy. I have never been much of a cook, so any time my mom prepared food was good with me.

I was glad they were there but uncomfortable as I struggled to conceal my condition. By this point, I had a definite small protrusion that I covered as artfully as possible. I was nervous that my mother would notice my weight gain, but she did not. I kept out of her view as much as possible and found a comfortable spot on the couch, draped with a blanket, while she bustled about in the kitchen. My dad and my sister were not my primary concern—only my mother would notice changes.

A loose sweatshirt and the fact that I could still fit into my jeans, albeit with the zipper and button open, made joining them at the table do-able. I am not sure how I managed to look normal and calm. Perhaps I didn't. Perhaps being somewhat weird was my norm. In any case, I escaped scrutiny.

That night, I gave up my bedroom to my parents and my sister while I slept on the couch. In billowing pajamas, I felt better, and I was grateful to be alone. As I settled down onto the narrow width of the couch, I turned onto my side and exhaled relief with a heavy sigh. I lie there thinking of my parents and my sister down the hall. They were so close. I could have opened the door and told them everything. I could have blurted out that I was pregnant and scared and sorry and ashamed and needed them. It was as close as the words that I might have uttered out loud. I wondered how they would they react. Would they be up-set, shocked, disappointed? Would it ruin my graduation ceremony the next day? Would the celebration be subdued and strained? Would my parents worry that they had to return home with difficult news instead of elation? Would they worry what people might say about me? ("All that money and education and now she's knocked up like the rest of them. She's no better and certainly no smarter for all the big shot uni-versity education she's got.")

I could not tell them. I had not said a word to anyone, not even Rob. I had to tell him and see what we might do together. I needed to see my doctor and confirm the pregnancy. No, with my graduation the next day, I decided to carry on pretending that things were normal. I had to keep my head together and graduate as planned. No drama.

It was on that night I felt the first movement of life. It came as a flutter, a gentle tickle inside the taut skin of my belly. On the narrow couch in the dark living room, under the covers, my hands shook as I placed them on my skin to feel my baby's first touch. It was an intimate moment that I shared with no one. With that movement, I sensed a little boy, real and vital. Life within me. A child with a heartbeat all his own, a heart that beat so close to mine during the time I carried him. As I felt him stir, I became his mother. My mother love tied me to him with an unfailing, unending bond. It awakened in me that night and has never left me.

In the morning, I put on my grey and pink graduation dress. It hung straight from the shoulders to the knee and had a thin belt that I buckled at the first hole to make a slight curve at the waist. I had tried on a pile of dresses before settling on this one. I took heaps of dresses into change rooms, struggling in and out of them, swearing and sweating. It's not easy to cry silently in a change room when you are frustrated. You want to scream it out. But I sat on a chair with dresses falling around me as I cried into my hands to muffle the sound. I was afraid that no dress would hide my condition. In the end, the grey and pink dress was the best of the lot. It looked like an old lady dress to me: I hated the colour, the style and the fabric. But it had to do. I was possibly the only girl who could not wait to put her graduation gown overtop my dress, which I did before I joined my parents to leave for the ceremony. That black, generous gown hid me inside. Thank God.

Graduation took place at the St. John's Arts and Culture Centre on the university grounds. It was a sunny day, crisp and perfect for hats, gowns and photos. We arrived on campus as graduates, and parents came from all directions in a sea of flower bouquets and excitement. I escorted my parents and sister to the auditorium and then headed to meet Rob in the graduate staging area.

When I found him, he was agitated. He hesitated, and then reluctantly relayed that his dad had given him money to cover the cost of our dinner that evening, but his family did not want to join us. I knew what that meant. His parents were not comfortable being with my parents. It felt like a slight. We argued, and Rob got angrier and angrier with me until I burst into tears, making him even angrier. We stood like that, fighting, with our backs to the other students. Finally, he softened and suggested that it would be more enjoyable to have dinner without his parents along anyway. I knew he was right, but it hurt me, and I could not ignore the way I felt.

With puffy, red eyes I left him to go find my place in line. I was near the front since I was receiving an honours degree. It meant that I would be on stage early in the ceremony, with my puffy eyes in full view. I sucked in my hurt feelings and pulled myself together. A little lipstick. A round of deep breaths. An effort to focus on the good of the day allowed me to walk into the auditorium with the other graduates as "Pomp and Circumstance" chorused us in. I have never been able to hear that music without feeling sad and a little sick. It reminds me of that day, when underneath the expected joy was pain that pulsed like a sonofabitch.

The ceremony went by in a blur. When my turn came, I managed to stand and walk up the stairs and across the stage without fainting or falling. The hood was placed over my head and onto my shoulders, and I returned to my seat with my degree in hand. If something poignant or meaningful was shared in the speeches, I missed it. I just wished it would end. When it did, I attempted to join in, offering congratulations and hugs, but unlike the students around me, I was not elated.

When the ceremony ended, we stood beside Burton's Pond and took the requisite proud family photos. I smiled. My parents remarked on what a great day it was, with the sun shining. I nodded.

My real graduation story is what was not said that day—that I was pregnant. Sad. I looked around me at those who were laughing, hugging and cheering for the camera, throwing their caps in the air. The jubilance of graduation was lost to me. Then, to top off the day, I went to dinner with Rob and my family, his family pointedly absent.

My older sister joined us at the restaurant. The chatter moved away from graduation, which was fine with me. The less I was noticed, the better. That day, I began practicing the art of acting okay when I wasn't. Somehow, in my mind, it was logical to think I was protecting my family by leaving them out of my situation. Why ruin their happiness along with mine?

I had a new job as a contract writer for an engineering firm in downtown St. John's. In my parents' eyes, I was making good on their investment in my education. I wanted to preserve that belief. I did not yet have a plan in place, but for that day, I let my family believe that I was the success I said I would be. And they were proud of me for it.

moored in a fen
of regrets
things I can't forget
bogged in
thick and deep
in a salty marsh
of tears
swamped and stranded
my heart upended
I cling to a boat
and float

Preg test!

Graduation over, I needed to visit my doctor. I had to get medical confirmation and attention, although confirmation seemed a moot point by then. I delayed making the appointment a couple more weeks but eventually braced myself and did the inevitable. Knowing I was pregnant, and well along, I was concerned that there were things I should be doing, or not doing. I worried I might have health matters that could impact the pregnancy, the child and me. Up until then, I had told myself that women had had babies for thousands of years without doctors. There was nothing to worry about—except, what if there was something to worry about?

I took the bus across town to my doctor's office. I sat in the waiting room preoccupied with what I would say once I was in the examination room. What words could I use to describe my situation to my doctor that would not make me seem certifiably crazy?

"Hey, I have this large swelling on my stomach, and I am not sure, but I think it might be a baby."

Or, "Hi, I have missed my period since, like, January and now my stomach is swollen."

Anything that came into my head was asinine and useless. I decided to stop deliberating and wait to see what came out of my mouth when my doctor walked into the examination room. Not a plan, but a good delay tactic.

I looked around the waiting room where little kids played among mothers with newborn babies in their arms. My insides churned from the stress and discomfort. On the wall, colourful posters showed the size of a fetus at the various stages of pregnancy. Fat, healthy babies suspended in cutaway profiles of the female body. Pretty pictures of babies with chubby cheeks and wide, sparkling eyes. Sitting there, I was sure that my bathroom Jesus was back and playing a joke on me, pushing these images in my face while he watched me cringe. I sat trying to seem nonchalant, separate from pregnancy, babies and new mothers. The possibility of fainting was very much a concern.

When my name was called, I made my way back to the examining room, and the nurse asked the reason for my visit. I lied and said I was there for abdominal pain. She eyed me suspiciously. I looked away. She left, closing the door behind her. In the small, silent room I endured the last moments of my secret life. I resumed my rehearsals of what to say when my doctor came in, trying to make the voice in my head sound upbeat and chipper. I willed myself to remain calm. Half of me was anxious for the relief that would come with the admission of what I had been hiding for the previous four months. The other half wanted to jump out the window and run, not looking back.

I was under the assumption that my doctor would judge me. She would know that I was having sex. Unmarried sex. She struck me as a woman with high morals. I was showing up on this day to admit my morals had gone down the toilet along with my prayers to Jesus and gads of toilet paper. My need to explain came from my lack of confidence and from what I saw as a delusional hope that my doctor would not judge me a loose hussy who had had unprotected sex and gotten pregnant. Yet, that is precisely how I saw myself as I waited for her. Loose. Hussy. Pregnant.

She breezed in the door, the floral skirt under her crisp white lab coat interrupting the silence with a swish. She stood across the room from me, in front of the window. The sun coming in through the shades outlined her form and made it difficult to see her face clearly.

"What can I do for you today?" she said, a smile in her voice.

I don't know what I said. I think I mumbled something about my stomach, missing periods and possibly being pregnant. She did not hesitate. She moved swiftly to the exam table, opened a drawer underneath and pulled out a paper sheet that she placed on top. She told me to remove my clothes from the waist down, including my underwear, and get under the sheet. She said this as she walked towards the door, smiling kindly. She explained that she would be back in five minutes to examine me. As quickly as that, actions in motion. No hesitation.

Alone again, I took in that word—examine. She was going to "examine" me. Within five minutes, she would see my stomach and its protruding bump. There would be no more pretending. I undressed and hurriedly folded my clothes into a neat pile on a chair, making sure to discreetly hide my underwear.

I climbed up on the table and unfolded and spread the flimsy, rattling paper sheet over the lower half of my body. I did not want my doctor bursting in on my half-naked self, despite the fact she would pull the sheet off me anyway. I sat there, bolt upright, with the sheet tucked under my bottom in a futile attempt at modesty. The door swung open once more, and my doctor politely ordered me to lie down. Brisk and focused, she peeled off the paper sheet. Then she placed her hands on my skin, feeling over and around and underneath the bulge. She produced a tape that she used to measure from the base of my ribcage to the top of my pelvic bone. I looked up at her face, and she beamed a broad, open smile as she nodded down at me. I was confused. Where were the judgement and admonishment? Where was the moralizing? The "What have you been up to, young lady?! And you not even married!"

Instead, she said, "My dear, you are at least twenty-two weeks pregnant."

Her exclamation rang into the room. "Really?" I responded, trying to sound surprised but not ridiculous, unable to accomplish either. She nodded with excitement, inserting the earpieces of her stethoscope before placing the other end on my round belly.

She smiled again and said, "There it is! A strong, healthy heartbeat!"

Without asking, she pushed the ends of the stethoscope into my ears, telling me to listen. My response? Tears. And then the words, "I can't be pregnant." It was not so much a wish as an admission that my situation was undesired and secret and had drained me in the months it had taken to get to that examination room. For the first time, I let myself cry a deep, real cry. I could not stop it. It no longer mattered to me what my doctor was thinking.

She stood for a moment with her hands gently on me as I sank into despair.

She kindly squeezed my hand and said, "You are going to have a baby. It's the most natural, wonderful thing in the world."

I looked at her, unable to respond or agree. My secret was now shared with her. We two were women alone in a room with my fate a known fact between us. I saw pity and concern in her eyes, and I looked away. I would have been better able to deal with admonishment.

She remained silent beside me for a few moments until I settled myself. Then she said, "Let me show you what the fetus looks like at twenty-two weeks. You are over half way there!"

I am not sure if she meant that as encouragement or felt a responsibility to provide the facts and status of my pregnancy. She left the room and then rushed back with a pamphlet that she unfolded to point to a fetus.

The appointment ended with her explaining that I had to go to the Grace Hospital lab for a pregnancy test. When I protested, saying she had already confirmed it, she responded that it was required. She urged me to go immediately since the hospital was only a block away and I would have it over and done with all in the same day. She also asked me to book regular appointments with her and gave me a prescription for vitamins that she said I should have been taking since I first became pregnant. There it was. One of the things that I should have been doing for my health and the baby's health but did not know about because I'd been in hiding.

My doctor's kindness was cursory and efficient, but still, I wanted to stay with her in that examination room. With one hand on the door, looking over her shoulder as she hurried out, she said she would see me soon. I'd let her see me at my most vulnerable, and she stood by stoically, waiting for me to calm down. I longed for her compassion, but she was gone.

I sat immobile for a few minutes taking in what had just happened. Vitamins. Pregnancy test. Prenatal. Twenty-two weeks pregnant. And a heartbeat. Inside my body was a living soul with a heartbeat. Not a swollen belly. Or missed periods. Or I might be pregnant. A baby was inside me with a head, body, legs, arms, little hands, tiny toes and a heartbeat. A strong, steady, beautiful heartbeat—that I'd heard.

Suddenly there was no space between me and my situation. I was having a baby, and that baby was growing inside me. I felt the sun on me as I sat half-undressed on the examination table thinking about these things, no longer caring that the door might open, that someone might discover me partially naked. I looked at the slant of the afternoon sun as it came in through the blinds, warm and hopeful on my bare legs. I desperately wanted to be warm and hopeful.

I dressed slowly, rousing the will to go to the lab for the pregnancy test. I looked in the mirror to check my face. Bloodshot, swollen eyes. I splashed water on my face and patted it dry with rough paper towels. I finally opened the door to go back down the hall to reception to make my next appointment. The scene in the waiting room was much as it had been when I left. Moms and kids and a few older people waiting to see the doctor. A regular day in my irregular world. People looked up at me as I walked into the room. I kept my head down, and my eyes averted. I made the appointment and left, stepping out into the sun, not knowing what was ahead except that in another eighteen weeks or so I would give birth. Whatever way I got there, that was the definitive outcome.

As I walked the block to the hospital, a new dread arose in me. Rob's father was a doctor at that hospital. What if I ran into him? I composed a story in my head about bloodwork, which was in fact true. If he pressed for more, I thought to tell him that it was part of my annual checkup. I got to the hospital and entered, my heart pounding, hoping not to see Rob's father or anyone else I knew. In the elevator, I hit B for the basement, where my doctor had said the lab was located. I found the door and opened it to find a waiting room full to capacity with patients. Damn! I thought this day could not get worse.

I excused my way through feet and purses to the check-in desk. I slid my doctor's note through the small, round opening of the glass in front of the receptionist. She was a large, no-nonsense looking woman typing forcefully on an electric typewriter. Her ample bosom bulged from her tight sweater and white lab coat. She did not look up or greet me as I stood self-consciously waiting. Finally, she took the order from my doctor and then peered at me over the top of her glasses and asked for my MCP card. I fumbled in my purse and slid it to her.

She rolled her chair back to a desk drawer behind and produced a small bottle. She rolled back towards me, bottle in her out-stretched hand and very loudly said, "Take this to the bathroom in the hallway. Pee into it and then return it here to me."

I took the container from her and stared at it. Seeing my hesitation, she loudly explained, "Go to the bathroom, sit on the toilet and when your urine starts, squeeze and halt the flow. Place the bottle down there and then let your pee stream into it until it is almost full." She spoke as if I was a child, her tone impatient. I was sure everyone in the waiting room had heard and was staring at me. Why did this woman have to be so loud, and so damn rude?

Another level of worse.

Head down, I turned and made my way back across the waiting room to find the bathroom. I managed to get most of the pee in the right place, cringing as some splashed onto my hand. I was shaking so badly it was unavoidable. I finished and washed the sealed container and my hands several times. I returned to the waiting room with it tightly concealed in my hand. I went all the way up to the desk and waited for the receptionist to acknowledge me once more. She grimaced a fake smile and reached out through the tiny opening to take the bottle. She told me I was free to go. They would call my doctor with the results.

I made my way one last time to the exit at the back of the room. Just as I reached the door, she called out in a booming voice for all to hear, "Preg test!"

I wanted the floor to open up and swallow me whole. I kept my head down and my gaze fixed on my shoes. I dared not look at anyone, still afraid that someone might recognize me. I swayed towards the door, yanked it open and bolted. The long hallway to the elevator was a blur. Out on the street, I hurried to the bus stop, thankful to be free and grateful not to have met anyone I knew, at least.

The day was sunny and warm. It was the sort of June day that should have encouraged me with the promise of summer. I did not care. I wished it was raining to match my misery. I would have preferred a day where I could hide under an umbrella and disappear inside it. The sun mocked my grey mood; I thought about how people say that it surprises them how life goes on, the sun keeps coming up, even when they are sad and lost. That's how it was for me. Sad and lost. The sun shone on me but not for me.

I got on the bus and collapsed into a seat. I would be home in a half hour. And then I would have to tell Rob. I would have to reveal what had been unspoken between us and make him face it with me. I wished for the bus ride to never end. I considered staying on indefinitely, riding loops of the city until I was forced off. I stared out the window, seeing familiar streets where I was now an outsider, a stranger in a place where I was no longer welcome. I was a new graduate with a degree that was supposed to stand for accomplishment and scholarship, yet I felt like a failure and a fraud. Everything I'd worked for was sidelined, completely overshadowed by the baby inside me.

An elderly lady behind me leaned forward and said, "What lovely hair you have." I turned to look over my shoulder at her. She was a grey-haired granny wearing a cheerful blue coat and matching hat. She clutched a shiny black purse on her lap. Her small, soft face lit with a generous smile as she looked in my eyes. I tried to smile back and muttered, "Thank you," then turned away.

Lovely hair! Why did old ladies on buses say crap like that, I wondered? Kindly and sweet as she was, I wished to be unnoticed. I thought of my own grandmother, who had died in 1979. If she had been alive, I might have had the courage to tell her I was pregnant. She and I were a pair. We had a likeness that drew me to share with her things I revealed to no one else. But she was long gone. I should have been nice to the old lady on the bus but what I wanted was to be left alone. Reminding me of my grandmother only made my situation seem more unbearable. I leaned close to the window and focused on becoming invisible. I could not do nice or normal or courteous. I could not abide sweet old ladies.

when the day
leaves me
at the shallow end
standing
in thoughts of regret
fretting
over what was said
and done
as if I was the one
who needed
to change
and rearrange myself
to fit your image
of retribution
giving you
absolution
I wade in further
then drift away
to a place
of empty silence
and absence
of you

telling

I had left my apartment in a nervous state and was returning even more agitated. My hiding place where I could no longer hide. I had a prescription in my purse for prenatal vitamins. I had an appointment card for my next prenatal visit. I had a lab test on order. I had a possible delivery date. I had endured the lab waiting room and the "preg test." I was outed.

I walked down the hall and into my bedroom with my coat still on. I caught sight of myself in the full-length mirror, pale, my eyes still puffy. I looked at my hair, thinking about how it appealed to old ladies who rode the bus in the middle of the day. The thought depressed me.

My bedroom had always been my place of comfort, here, in my dorm room and at home with my parents. It was where I cried over jerk boyfriends, cruel gossip and idiotic mistakes. It was where I spent quiet time thinking and figuring out problems. It was my retreat, my think-ing, dreaming, planning, weeping, "deal with it and get over it" space.

I sat on the bed and pulled the phone from the nightstand onto my lap. How to make the call? What to say? This call would end one reality and begin another. Would he pick up? Would he be in a meeting? I dialled the number to his office and waited several rings until he answered. Without even saying hello or caring if he was free, I asked him to come to my apartment. No discussion, just that he needed to come right away. He said yes, and we hung up.

For the ten minutes that it took him to get there, I waited on the bed with my coat and shoes still on. I sat with my breath and my heartbeat in the otherwise silent room, knowing exactly what I would say when he arrived, but unable to predict his response. I did not dare to hope. I kept my thoughts entirely on the words, "I'm pregnant."

I heard the door open. He came and stood in the bedroom doorway, looking at me expectantly, not speaking. I let the words "I'm pregnant" tumble out, fear and relief rising in me in equal measure. I was afraid he would be angry. Yet I was relieved to finally admit what I had known for months and what I was sure he had known as well. I searched his face and found not anger but instead a slight smile, a smirk of recognition, perhaps. I blurted out that he could leave me if he wanted to. That I was ready for that. He was quiet and still.

Then he dryly said, "No. We can take care of this."

For one second, I dared to hope that he wanted our child. That he was happy. That he would throw his arms around me and hug me, tell me everything would be wonderful. That he would marry me, and we would live happily ever after. The three of us.

But the second passed and he went on about a friend of his who recently had an abortion, how easy it was. I would have to go to New York, but that would not be a problem. He would pay for it. No one would need to know. He was pacing. Thinking. Planning.

He did not reach for me or touch me. He just stood there solving the problem out loud while I fell into the shock, sliding down into the place inside me where there was nothing but the sound of my heart. One loud beat after another, drumming into my head. It made me wonder how life could go on in a steady rhythm even after you are sure it is ending. There was no compassion. No tenderness. Not one inkling of hope.

I looked at him and did not know him. Even though our relationship would continue for some years after that day, my love for him shattered in those few moments. Resentment crept in and settled down between us, ultimately destroying any chance we had of a life together. His desire to hide the pregnancy and get rid of the problem came from fears in him that I did not, and could never, fully understand. But what I knew from that conversation was that love, if indeed he loved me, was not enough.

I knew long before that moment what his answer would be. I did not want to accept it, but I was sure of it. It existed in his avoidance and denial of what was happening in my body. It showed up in anger when he struck me with his hands and yelled in my face. It was apparent in the distance growing between us as he made plans that left me on the periphery. We had been skirting the issue, avoiding the truth that now moved inside me. It seemed to me that his answer was prepared, at hand for the moment I would finally say, "I'm pregnant." It's possible he had rehearsed it as he anticipated and waited for my admission.

When I'd rented a new apartment, the first of my own without a roommate, he showed no interest in moving in. More nights than not, he returned to his parents' house and left me alone. After four years together, we were still dating. Yet, on the bus ride home that day

I imagined what it would feel like to hear him say yes to a baby. I day-dreamed about him wrapping me up in his arms and dancing us all over the apartment to celebrate. I dared to hope that saying I was pregnant would unleash a flurry of happy emotions. He had a job. I had a job. We were university graduates and young professionals. We had the means to marry and have a child.

I was lost in these thoughts, remote and silent until he startled me by coming close to my face to refocus my attention on him. "Don't worry—abortion is not a big deal." I managed to croak out that I was already twenty-two weeks pregnant. I don't know if he understood what that meant, but it did not deter him from his plan.

He paced back and forth in my small bedroom, seemingly energized by the situation presented to him. I sat motionless, listening. The months the pregnancy went unacknowledged were more bearable than what was now happening. He did not want our child. I had been coping alone—now he was taking over and dictating what we would do. He wanted rid of the "problem." In a single conversation, hope was replaced with certain loss.

I don't recall how we finished the conversation. He eventually left to return to his office. After a long time, I stood to take off my coat and shoes.

I was weak. Young. I was afraid of him. Our relationship had taken on shades of abuse, although I did not put that label on it. Many years later, as our short marriage unravelled, a psychiatrist held up his hand to stop me as I described our relationship.

"You realize that you are describing a classic case of abuse?"

I shook my head and said I wouldn't let someone abuse me. He leaned towards me and kindly said, "But you have. And you need to get out and stay out of that relationship."

He explained to me that statistics show that more women by far remain in abusive relationships than leave. I stayed for many years. I did not ever call it abuse; it was a distasteful word in my mouth. It embarrassed me. I did not want it attached to me. Yet, it applied. Perhaps women stay because they feel, as I did, that it cannot be true. They want to believe that love will ultimately fix the wrongs, the hurts and pain. They don't want to admit it could happen to them. We were upper-middle-class people from good families. I was naive enough to think that made a difference. I've learned since that abuse is an ugly reality across all classes, ethnicities, races and cultures.

The day I told Rob I was pregnant, I relinquished control to him. He grasped the power to determine much of what happened after that because I let it go that way. He had already gained the upper hand in our relationship. For me, being pregnant was one thing. I endured that. Having a child was another matter. It could have meant acceptance and taking up a new path together as parents. It could have meant that the pregnancy, while unplanned, translated into something beautiful and lasting. I wanted that future, not a New York back alley abortion. What I wanted was not what happened. Not that day or any day since.

*love she said
has eluded me
left me standing
at the side of the road
in the rain
without an umbrella
looking both ways
with my hands shoved deep
in my pockets
gripping a locket
tarnished and cheap
empty of photos
mocking my dream
of love*

unplanned unparenthood

The next day, Rob drove me to the Planned Parenthood office in his new Volkswagen Rabbit, the car that marked his transition from university into his career. When we pulled to a stop in the parking lot, I got out and looked around me. St. John's is a small city, and the office was at the apex of three streets, making it a focal point from each direction. I rushed us inside.

The building was a house that had been converted into offices. We entered a hallway at the bottom of a staircase, with no clear direction to a reception area. We walked around the corner and found a room filled with pamphlets, books and magazines depicting pregnancy, parenthood and birth choices. Makeshift furniture indicated modest funds and earnest intentions. It was quiet and serene, with muffled conversations coming from behind closed doors. The scent of brewed coffee hung in the air along with food odours that reminded me of organic granola.

A young woman came up behind us, bearing a coffee cup. She made her way to a small desk in the corner as she greeted us and asked us to take a seat. She confirmed our names and that we were there to see a counsellor. Rob and I sat together on a small couch, not speaking. On the drive over, we had not talked about what we were going to say. I knew from my doctor that abortion at this stage was impossible. I was there to let him discover for himself what I already understood.

Much of that visit remains a blur of apprehension and discomfort, but I vividly recall the kind, patient and respectful counsellor who took us into her office. She appeared to be one of St. John's granola crowd, people who shopped at Mary Jane's on Water Street and wore tie-dyed t-shirts and hemp skirts. Her stringy brown hair was tied in a loose ponytail, and there was no makeup on her plain but pleasant face. Her long, gauzy cotton skirt, floral-patterned blouse and soft-soled, practical leather shoes suited her. Her eyes were a warm brown that made her pretty when she smiled.

She greeted us warmly and led us to a small room with barely enough space for the three chairs we sat in. She was gracious and open but seemed to look at us with caution. She asked what brought us there. I described our situation. Pregnant. Twenty-two weeks. Here to inquire about abortion options.

She stopped me. "You are twenty-two weeks pregnant?"

Already embarrassed, I nodded in affirmation.

"You are too far along for an abortion. It is extremely high risk, and no regular doctor will take you. You would end up in a backstreet clinic in New York, and you could bleed out on the table. There would be no aftercare," she said, her voice serious and direct.

Rob interrupted her. Leaning toward her, he said, "But it is still possible? How much would it cost?"

We both looked at him incredulously.

She turned abruptly to me, squaring her chair with mine so we were eye to eye. "You do not want to do this. You are too far along. You might die on the table." She placed her hands on my arms and continued to look at me. I felt her warmth and the urgency in her touch. She seemed to be willing strength into me to stand up for myself. I am sure she saw a young, fresh-faced, scared girl who was deep in trouble and whose boyfriend did not know or was denying the gravity of his request. She did not bother to give him an answer or even look at him. She made me promise before we left that I would under no circumstances consider an abortion. She pressed more pamphlets into my hands with pictures of the fetus at twenty-two weeks. I can still see her face. I can still feel the imprint of her concern.

We left, silent. We drove in silence until, looking straight ahead, I said, "I won't do it. I won't have an abortion."

He said nothing. He did not argue or try to convince me otherwise.

Those were the days of Dr. Henry Morgentaler and his fight to legalize abortion clinics where women could receive dignified care instead of risking their lives in backstreet operations. It would not be until 1988 that women in Canada could somewhat freely choose abortion. A committee of doctors decided if a woman could abort her pregnancy. Morgentaler opened his Toronto clinic in June of 1983, the same month I visited Planned Parenthood in St. John's. But choice was still not widely supported, certainly not in Newfoundland. "Pro-life" was the subject of sermons across Canada and the United States. Morgentaler was still seen by many to be doing the work of the devil, taking life away, killing unborn babies. Unplanned pregnancy was the fate of girls and women who had not made the godly choice, abstinence. Pregnancy was penance, and few seemed to care much about the mental, emotional and physical well-being of the fallen. It seemed to me that people were eager to judge and condemn and even more eager to decide the fate of girls pregnant out of wedlock.

I followed Morgentaler and the stories of his clinics, eventually finding my own voice and opinions in the debate. I am grateful to him and all the women who struggled for choice and won. I am so grateful that my daughter lives in a time when birth control is openly available. She will not endure the same kind of judgement women of earlier generations did, and she will decide when and if she has children.

But I grew up in Newfoundland, in a time and place where pregnancy meant you had the baby. Some were sent away from their communities and families. It was considered to be in the girl's best interest, not to mention family members who hoped to save face, particularly with the church crowd. When she came home, everyone knew where she had been. But they didn't talk to her. They talked about her.

"Yes, my dear, she got herself in trouble. No sense to these young ones. Too young to know what they're getting into. They sent her away to have it and get rid of it. Now here she is back like nothing happened. Must be shockin' awful for her poor mother."

No counselling or support; just whispers and ridicule. And the boys? Never their fault: "Boys will be boys." They could do as they pleased with as many girls as they wanted. When one of those girls got pregnant, the boy stepped out of view while she bore the shame and a life with a buried secret, one that sleeps and rises with her. In the book *Shantaram,* by Gregory David Roberts, I found these lines that eloquently sum up what it means to carry this kind of pain. "But some feelings sink so deep into the heart that only loneliness can help you find them again. Some truths about yourself are so painful that only shame can help you live with them. And some things are just so sad that only your soul can do the crying for you."

Having a child and giving up that child is a level of loss, pain, shame and regret that is almost indescribable. The pain hunts you from within and never leaves you alone.

Some of the girls in our community had their babies and kept them. They gave up their youth. They lived with their parents. Many dropped out of school. Some married or moved in with the father, relationships that rarely survived. I saw these young mothers when I visited my hometown, pushing strollers, still dressed in the faded jeans and jackets of high school. They looked away, pretending not to see or know me, avoiding contact and unwanted conversation. Some of those girls made it work; sometimes, with the loving support of family and community, they established a good life. But there was little thought given to what it took for them to endure, overcome and go on.

These were the girls I had sworn never to become, those whose lives were rearranged by the arrival of a child, dreams replaced with the burden of unplanned responsibilities. Girls who raised their kids in households where they were still kids themselves, dependent on their parents—without an education, a career or even a home of their own.

These forlorn girls weighed heavily on me and the decision I made when my own child was born.

Would I have chosen abortion if it had been more accessible and acceptable? No. I knew that bringing my son into the world was the only right choice for me. From the moment I felt life within me, I knew. I did not get pregnant on purpose, but I gave life to my son with absolute purpose. He was meant to be in the world. I am proud that I had the strength to have him.

But I could not go back to my community with a baby and without a husband. I could not walk into a church that told me I was a sinner for having sex before marriage. I could not endure the support of people who would label me as an unwed mother and a failure, so Rob and I agreed to keep the pregnancy a secret and then give up my baby for adoption. I could not bring my son into that other kind of life.

That's how I saw it then and how I still see it—even though I now know that I was only guessing about how that life might have turned out for me and my son.

I
picked up
the pieces
on the floor
and saw in the
broken mirror
me
in shattered
matter
where once
I
was whole

mirror, mirror, on the wall

My small basement apartment was located on Thorburn Road, directly across from the Avalon Mall. It was a busy street with all-day traffic, buses, trucks, cars and people. The house was a three-bedroom bungalow like most others in the neighbourhood, with a basement made into a furnished one-bedroom apartment for extra income. A small staircase led down from the driveway to the apartment door on the lower, righthand side of the house.

Inside, the noise of Thorburn Road receded, but I found the furnishings depressing. They had belonged to the grandmother of the family upstairs, who had lived in the apartment until she died, something I felt was best not dwelled upon. There was a lot of gold brocade fabric from the seventies and the bedroom had twin beds that I pushed together to make into one. The bed, night table and dresser were all dark maple with brass drawer pulls, which matched the dark maple dining room table and four matching chairs. But at four hundred dollars a month, the price was right, and the location was good for transit to any part of the city. It was my first apartment. Not chic, but when I closed the door behind me it was mine, and I liked that.

In the hallway, there was a full-length mirror I passed whenever I made my way from the living room to the bedroom or bathroom. Each time, I was startled by the pregnant girl there. She had my hair, face, arms and legs, but her torso was not mine. I had to get used to her, to find a way to accept her. It was the mirror that introduced me to my pregnant self, the new self who grew out of and into my body.

I'd turn sideways to see my expanding middle. Wanting to know how other people saw me, I'd then twist to look over my shoulder. Did my butt look bigger? Or just wider? My waist had slowly squared and disappeared, and I took to wearing loose clothing. Remaining the same in the eyes of others was the impossible expectation of everything I wore. I worried that my body would never be the same again as women in my family complained of not being able to lose the "baby fat" that clung to their bellies and hips. Every day I worried about just how huge I would get, knowing there was not a thing I could do but watch myself grow.

Mirrors stop women all the time. We pause to check our hair, lipstick and clothes, to admire and critique. We are endlessly interested in how we are perceived. Looking in a mirror, we seldom exclaim with delight. More likely we see what needs fixing, what displeases. Examining my growing belly was an obsession. The day inevitably came, when with great alarm, I could no longer suck it in—in fact, sucking it in only made it protrude more. It was, I realized, the safe shell inside which my child was growing.

It happened suddenly. One day my favourite jeans abruptly caught on my thighs as I tried to pull them on. I danced and hopped until I managed to force them over my "not sure where they came from" fleshy hips. It seemed that overnight I had had a giant growth spurt and it was entirely on my lower half. The zipper gaped open in a huge V, my belly protruding like a misshapen muffin. I flopped onto the bed, defeated; trapped in my Levis. Red-faced and frustrated, I rolled around, swore and tugged them back off, flinging them into the bottom of my closet. I was officially fat!

I had seen the repulsive maternity jeans pregnant women wore. The jeans with a stretchy panel in the front and elastic waistbands, their butts lost inside the excess fabric that hung and sagged at the back. These were the women who proudly waddled, strutting their pregnancy. Mothers who walked in pairs, prattling overtop strollers. Mothers already married, established and building families. Mothers, who upon learning they were pregnant, celebrated the news with husbands and grandparents and friends. A joyful addition.

Not me. I was a secret-keeper. My pregnancy was not celebrated. I was not married or established or building a family. I was twenty-one and barely out of university. I was hiding my belly and not admitting to anyone, not even myself most days, that I was pregnant. So maternity jeans with stretchy panels were not coming to my wardrobe. Not a chance. I was also determined that those skinny jeans would be back to snug my young ass as soon as possible. In the meantime, I did not have a fucking clue what I was going to wear. (Where were yoga pants when I needed them?)

Keeping a secret that is growing out the front of your body is impossible. But that is in fact what I attempted. Being the skinny girl was not ideal for someone in my situation. A generous, fleshy body might have let me conceal pregnancy with more success. I had heard of heavier women going into labour without knowing they were pregnant, going to hospital complaining of severe cramps and coming out with a baby. I was ninety-five pounds when I got pregnant, a bit of a girl whose stomach was flat and whose breasts were buds barely requiring a bra. My dad used to tell me to eat every time he saw me. He would predict that a good gust of wind could blow me away. It was not the kind of body built to hide anything, least of all a growing abdomen. My profile quickly resembled a basketball on a stick.

I was in a love-hate relationship with that hallway mirror. I tried to not look yet could not look away.

Mirror, mirror on the wall, who's the thinnest of them all?

Not Mary, not anymore. Haha!!

Mirror, mirror on the wall, look who's pregnant after all.

For every girl I had ever ridiculed, for every slight, for every time I had uttered "not me," this was payback. What we put out comes back to us and often with a force more powerful. Good or bad.

At first glance, my reflection in the mirror showed the baby bump. But I had to get intimate with the mirror to see what was even more altered. Up close, face to face, I stared into my wide, brown eyes and there was she was—my scared, scarred self.

Perhaps I was never innocent.

Perhaps the bump on my torso was the truth pushing out, revealing who I was after all—a bad girl with secrets she wished not to tell.

Perhaps I faced myself in the mirror in brave solitude to see not my reflection, but who I was becoming.

I was my most honest self when no one was looking. I acknowledged my vulnerabilities and accepted them, my public facade put aside. In my small apartment, I accepted my changing body. I took off my clothes and stood naked before the mirror. I slid my hands over my firm round belly and breasts. I considered my body and its mystery. I cried for the girl I used to be and offered love to the one who replaced her. I was not bad. I was beautiful. In private, I became this new me and knew I was more than the fear that gripped me when I stepped out the door. I was a woman with a child in her womb. I was sensual, voluptuous and richly alive in my curvaceous body. There in my solitary space I was okay. Almost safe.

Mirror, mirror on the wall, who is the fairest one of all?

As I see her now, she is the one brave enough to tell her tale. She is a survivor. She is the one who took a fall but could not be kept down, who discovered she had courage and grit and resolve. She is the one with a fire in her that could not be extinguished, the one you see now, walking down the street with a swing in her hips that speaks of confidence.

She is the one you can trust with your secrets because she knows about carrying things within. Unbearable things. She is the one you want on your side through rough times because she has the calm and the resources to pull you through.

She is the one who is just like you. Don't be fooled by her poise.

She had to work for that. She went to the beastly underbelly and fought for it. She stood where you are standing now. She faced what you are facing. She has in her what you seek and need. She is the one that the mirror never forgets because her reflection is not just the face of loveliness but the soul of strength. She is me. The me that I became.

It took me a long time to gain my confidence and claim my power. Getting up close to the mirror in my hallway, peering into my eyes, it was difficult to see who I would become. The twenty-one-year-old girl with bright brown eyes looked back at me and occasionally even smiled. I pushed my auburn curls away from my face and pressed my forehead to the cool glass. That me in the mirror was my closest friend, my only friend. To me she was the fairest one of all because she lived with me through the dark days, the silent ones, the ones that echoed and replayed. I did it one day at a time by summoning courage from a store deep down that I did not know was there until I needed it. It was not a fairy tale, but a tale all the same. And I was my own hero.

Prince Charming was nowhere to be found, his rescue not offered, and in the end, not needed.

*the past
crept in around her
stirring old feelings
long suppressed
and suddenly
without warning
she was crying
for what was lost
with the passage
of time*

upstairs-downstairs

Except for work, I stayed in my basement apartment that summer. Upstairs lived the family I rented from—Mom, Dad and two sons. They were friendly but never intrusive. They left me alone. There was a yard at the back of the house that the mom encouraged me to use. She said I could pull out a sun chair from the shed and sit out there any time I wanted. She had said that to me as summer began to blossom, long before the weather was warm enough or my pregnancy advanced enough to notice. I never once sat in the yard.

From my bedroom or dining room window I could see the kids in the yard with their little dog. My view at eye level was of their feet running through the grass, the dog chasing close at their heels. At times their voices and laughter were comforting, adding a quality of normality. I came and went from the side entrance, so the backyard was just a view out my windows. I let them think me shy, reclusive, reluctant. In my head, I created conversations, imagined them speculating about the weird girl who lived downstairs as they passed the potatoes and beef during dinner. I imagined them saying, "There is a secret there," as they raised their assuming eyebrows. But maybe they did not think about me at all or even wonder what I was doing. Perhaps, I thought, they had more interesting things than their lonely tenant to talk about over dinner.

The mom, I became certain, had figured out that I was pregnant. Once when I was passing her my monthly rent cheque, I caught her looking at my stomach quizzically. She looked up at me with that mom look of concern. "If there is anything you need, you let me know," she said. I winced but politely declined, saying I was fine, laughing my nervous laugh. Her eyes held on to me briefly.

Women feel each other like that. We say more in a look than we can with words. I could see in her face what I had seen in my mother's face at times. That look of seeing me into my head. I kept my eyes averted. I changed the subject, making benign comments on the weather. "What a great summer we are having, don't you think." She nodded. I thrust the rent cheque into her hand and walked away, leaving her standing in the doorway, her eyes still on me. Let her wonder, I thought, as my door closed and locked behind me.

At night I heard them moving about upstairs. The kids running. The mom corralling them for bed. A phone ringing. Laughter and conversations. I sat with a book, settled in bed, thankful there were people upstairs. Their noises were a comfort to me in my aloneness. I kept the mom's words about needing anything as a security option. The "what if" possibility, should I need help at some point. I hoped not, and it never came to that, but it was good to think help was directly above me. They were good people. Middle-class and hard-working.

I imagined going up there, knocking on the door and asking if I could speak with her. I saw the two of us sitting on her couch as I told her what was happening to me. I imagined her holding my hand, maybe hugging me. She and I might shed tears together as she sympathized with me over my situation. But even though I knew she was earnest in her offer to help, I could not imagine how she could. She was not my mother. Not my family. Not even a friend. She was my landlord. I was her tenant. To confide in her was a risk. Telling her might have made me feel less alone, but outside of that, what could she have done? Urged me to go to my parents? She was a mother but not my mother. It was my mother I wanted, and my mother she would have urged me to reach out to.

I listened in the mornings to hear them leave. Once the house was quiet, I would get my coat and shoes on and leave as well. I took the bus downtown to my job at the engineering firm where I worked as a writer and editor. I sat in an office that overlooked the harbour, reading, editing and rewriting long pages of dry, boring engineering documents filled with technical terms and specifications. I enjoyed being in a professional setting. I felt like an adult with a real job in the adult world. At lunch, on the days I felt able to brave being outside, I ate lunch on the steps of the National War Memorial, people-watching to pass the hour. On most days, I ate my lunch at my desk. I was beginning to show enough that I hesitated to make too many public appearances, although the sun and warm air won out occasionally.

That June, Prince Charles and Princess Diana came to St. John's aboard the Royal Yacht *Britannia* to mark the four-hundredth anniversary of Newfoundland becoming a British colony, the first colony in the British Empire. They docked almost directly in front of my office building. It seemed everyone was at the harbour to greet them as they disembarked, me among them. I'd stepped out from my office determined to see Princess Diana up close, in person. She was born on July 1, 1961, and I was born on September 11 of the same year. Like the rest of the world, I was enamoured with her.

She was beautiful and shy, gracious and lovely. For a moment I caught her eye and she smiled at me. That moment was incredibly special for me. In the years that followed, her secrets and sadness were revealed, her dysfunctional marriage and the loneliness she endured. As she stood up to the royals and claimed her life and her escape, she was a role model for me. She remains an inspiration.

As a Newfoundlander, I grew up with "God Save the Queen" on my lips and the Queen's portrait on our kitchen wall at home. To see the prince and princess was a rare privilege. I stood there thinking about Diana and how I wished I could talk to her as a woman of my age. I might have leaned in further to let her grasp my hand had I not been fearful that the television cameras might be on me. She and I were both twenty-one, worlds apart and yet both on a path that would teach us who we were and what we were capable of. I so wanted to see her happy, flourishing with her children, and her death in 1997 affected me profoundly.

I walked back to my office grateful for that brief encounter. Countless days go by and are readily forgotten, but a few moments can so impress you that they leave you transformed for the better. That morning I stepped into Diana's light and left it with a bit of hope that I held in my heart for times when I needed it most. She had a presence that I took in to carry with me. She made me think that 1961, the year she was born, was a special year in the history of the world. I was glad I'd been born in it too.

My work that summer was tedious. It was an office of mostly men, engineers, and a smattering of women who were the administrative support. I avoided the women because they eyed me suspiciously, with my loose jackets over shapeless dresses. I liked having a big desk to hide behind and I kept my head down, busy and preoccupied. When the end of the day came, I let the others leave before I gathered up my things to go home. While the material I was working on was a bit of a slog, I took delight in making it read well. It was pleasing to know that what I was editing would be published and I would have been a part of making it ready.

I took the bus home in the evening with equal parts relief and dread. I looked forward to changing into comfortable clothes, being able to relax while making something to eat in my little kitchen. I'd put a cassette into my ghetto blaster and sing along with Prince or Michael Jackson as I prepared dinner. But the evening also meant being alone with my thoughts. Or being with Rob, who would pull up to the house on his motorcycle, full of an energy that annoyed me. His social life continued without me. I resented it but, having agreed to our plan of concealing the pregnancy and giving up our child, I didn't feel that I could complain. I endured the time alone. It felt like a prison sentence where I was the prisoner as well as the warden.

Out of sight. Safe from view. Alone. I told myself it was necessary, to avoid social disgrace. I locked out the world, pulled down the shades, turned out the lights. My thoughts grew dark at times. Imaginings and possibilities haunted me. If I had gone upstairs and told the woman upstairs what was happening to me downstairs, I believe the telling would have released me from my self-imposed prison. But I chose not to tell. I stayed hidden downstairs while upstairs remained a knock away and as distant as another land.

If I had the chance now, I would go back there, knock at her door and ask her what she knew. I would tell her that I took comfort in having her and her family close to me. Without knowing it, they were a source of support, more than anyone else that summer. I would sit with her and tell her the truth. Yes, we might cry and talk about what might have happened if I had told her at the time. But mostly I would be grateful to tell her how I appreciated her. I would tell her that in the summer of 1983, when I was pregnant and scared in her downstairs apartment, I was grateful that she and her family were upstairs. In fact, they were the only access to family that I had.

I am

the storm upon the page

words

raining down in a rage

riotous thunder

and flashing light

that splits the night

of terrors

until my wicked pen

is spent

and I can safely open

a window

to greet the sun's consolation

of calm

now that the storm

has passed through me

and set me

free

Walmart was a big enough store, I reasoned, that I wouldn't be noticed. I could find the things on my list, get in and out without worrying about running into someone familiar. No one I knew shopped there, especially in the early morning. It would be mostly old ladies shuffling idly about while their husbands gathered for a yarn on the benches out in the mall. In a few hours I was leaving for the airport and a "home for unwed mothers" in Halifax. I would be out of Newfoundland and out of view. I would escape and not a single person in the province except me, Rob and my doctor would ever know I was pregnant. I made my way to the personal care aisles. No browsing—my mission was to be done and out of there as quickly as possible.

With a small basketful of toiletries, I hurried to the checkout. The ring of cash registers and benign conversations of women in the line lulled me into my own thoughts. I was running through my mental list of tasks to complete before I left for the airport. There was not a lot to pack, since this was in no way a vacation. Several books, my Sony Discman and the few loose maternity-like clothes that I owned were the only real priorities. Oh, and something to wear home after it was all over. I was not sure I had anything that would fit my post-delivery body, but I would throw something in and hope for the best.

Reluctant to emerge from the comfort of my private thoughts, I was slow to notice the person calling out to me. It was a girl Rob and I knew from university. We had intersected from time to time through our social circles, at campus parties and downtown bars. Not a close friend—but close enough to remember me, to know my name. Too close. Too good a memory.

"Mary! Mary! Hi, Mary! Over here!"

I looked at her but turned away abruptly, pretending not to see her. She was waving at me, smiling and leaning forward to get closer. Her insistence made me instantly afraid of being found out despite my perfect track record up to that moment. If she got nearer, she would see my protruding belly. It now August. My job had ended a couple of weeks ago and I was no longer able to go out in public without draping my paunchiness in man-sized sweatshirts or moo-moo dresses and over-sized jackets.

Panic rose. My heart was pounding; sweat formed under my arms and trickled down into small of my back. The checkout girl slid my soap, shampoo and razors across the scanner, looking with bemused interest from me to the girl at the back of the line. I pushed twenty dollars into her hand and grabbed a shopping bag, shoving my items inside, desperately trying to speed up the transaction. The cashier did not respond to my urgency—she seemed determined to move at a glacial pace, maybe out of curiosity. I wanted to slap her. I wanted to slap someone! I needed to get the hell out of that line and be gone.

I would not look back. I would not acknowledge the girl calling my name. People were staring but I did not look back. I held out my shaking hand and grabbed my change. Then I stumbled towards the exit. The girl had now left the line and was following me. I quickened my step, practically running. As I pulled open the double-glass door she called out one last time.

"Mary, I see you. And I can see you're pregnant."

FUCK!!!!

Her words rang loud and clear. I heard an intonation of glee—she had caught me, and she knew it. I stood still, my heart pounding, my mouth open in disbelief. I fought my tears along with the urge to turn and tell her to mind her own fucking business.

Instead, I bolted. The doors of Walmart closed behind me. She did not follow. She had said what she wanted to say and made her point—in the most public of ways.

In my distress, I had come out the wrong exit and now had to walk the long way around the mall to cross the street to my apartment. I kept my head down and my package in front of me like a shield against further prying eyes. The August sun reflected unforgivingly off the concrete and pavement. I was hot and sweating and swearing under my breath.

How the fuck did this happen? How did this girl I barely knew show up at Walmart, of all places? Why was she there so early in the morning? Why did she yell out like that in front of strangers? Who did she know? Who would she tell? The questions pounded into my brain as I rushed on like a crazy woman, muttering and stumbling my way home.

FUCK!!!

I would deny it. I would say I never saw her. I would laugh like it was ridiculous that she thought it was me. It wasn't me. It wasn't FUCKING me!!

I kept swearing. I kept saying the F-word over and over. I could hear my mother's admonishment, telling me that swearing was hurtful to God and a sin. Another one! I was long past caring, and swearing was the only thing that felt good as I stumbled my way through the Avalon Mall parking lot.

My carefully planned trip to Walmart had come unraveled and me with it. I needed a drink in the worst way but could not have one. I needed a friend but there was no one I could call. Most of all, I needed my mother. I wanted to lean my head on her shoulder and have her say that everything would be all right. I wanted to give up and give in to my longing for the love that would soothe my weariness. I wanted to go home. I wanted to come out of hiding and walk around freely with my pregnancy in plain view. These thoughts unhinged what little composure remained. I fell into my apartment heaving great sobs, then locked the door behind me, shutting out the cruel drama.

I would be gone in a few hours, gone far from that girl and anyone else who knew me. What she thought she saw would be speculation. No proof available. No matter who she told it would remain a question mark. Gossip.

I never saw her again. I no longer recall her name and only vaguely remember what she looked like. If she told anyone I never heard. Perhaps I thought myself of more interest to others than I was.

I left St. John's behind that day on a flight to Halifax, to the place that would be my home for the next two months. It was both a risk and a triumph. My family thought I was going to Halifax for a job assign-ment. They did not ask questions or seem concerned. My doctor had encouraged me to tell my older sister what I was doing, but in the end, I couldn't do it. I had promised Rob that it was our secret. It's a short flight from St. John's to Halifax but it was a long way from my home to the home where I was about to reside. The Home of the Guardian Angel.

*imagine she said
yourself somewhere
beautiful
even as you stand
inside dread
give wings
to your hopes
even though
you are afraid to fly
this time
will pass you by
and someday
one day
the beautiful
will be your home*

The plan

Rob and I had agreed upon the Home of the Guardian Angel as the best option. A home for unwed mothers. Such as I was. We concocted the plan to tell family and friends that I was going to Halifax on assignment with the engineering company I'd worked with that summer. We explained we were not sure how long I would be gone, but two months was the likely time frame. A plausible plan to accommodate me being away until the baby was born and placed for adoption. Then I would return home with my supposed assignment complete. The business, so to speak, taken care of and behind us.

Sitting in my doctor's office, as we discussed this option, I had been hopeful in a hopeless way. There was no good solution. Rob had gone from abortion to adoption without any other consideration. We never once spoke of keeping the baby. He treated me as if I was not even pregnant and didn't ask how I was feeling or if I was okay. What he thought or worried about, I did not know.

One sultry summer afternoon, he came by my apartment with his motorcycle and wanted to take me for a ride. I thought it dangerous to be pregnant and riding a motorcycle, not to mention uncomfortable. Rob loved to drive fast on that bike. He leaned into the curves of the road and instructed me to lean with him. I understood the physics, but there was no way I wanted to try that pregnant. He asked me several times, but I refused until he gave up and left. That afternoon, while I napped on my bed, he was in an accident. An elderly lady in an Oldsmobile pulled out from a side road and he ran into her car, catapulting off the bike. He was saved by his helmet and leather gear, but the police said if there had been a passenger on the bike, that person would have been killed. That passenger would have been me.

It was that kind of young, wild freedom that he loved. I had loved that about him: His crazy let's-go, devil-may-care attitude. But now it left me alone with the weight of responsibility. I could no longer do what he wanted me to do. We could not engage socially. We could not go to the movies. I would not get on the back of his bike. Ironically, it was pregnancy that saved me that day. It was pregnancy that kept me home.

My doctor explained to me that the home was a well-run, reputable place for young girls who wanted care and guidance during their pregnancies. She sensed my discomfort when she mentioned it was a Catholic-run home and hastened to explain that it did not exclude girls of other faiths, or no faith. I was entirely unclear at the time where I stood on faith since Jesus and I were not on speaking terms and God seemed to have taken a vacation from my life. My doctor went on to say that she had sent a quite a few girls to the home with good results.

Good results? What were good results? They didn't die? They had their babies? Gave them up? Survived to tell the story? Was there a club to join afterwards? The unwed unsung mothers club?

I was listening to my doctor and preparing myself mentally to accept the label of unwed mother. One who would stay in a place called the Home of the Guardian Angel. A place operated by Catholic nuns, women who had given up sex to choose celibate lives, pure and free from the weak ways of the flesh. How could they have compassion for me, a wayward Protestant? Was this the way Jesus would answer my bathroom tirades?

My doctor carried on, but I could barely take in the details and forgot them immediately. She wrote down the information and pressed the paper into my hands, saying she would contact them to make my arrangements. I was to choose a date to go and book a flight. She smiled kindly at me and reassured me that it would work out for the best. She awkwardly put her hand on my shoulder in an attempt at encouragement as she made her way out the door. In the face of impending sadness and struggle, why do people always say that everything will work out for the best?

I felt very small. The little girl me wanted to be taken care of. I wanted to believe there was a magical place that I could go to where my troubles would disappear. I wished for a movie version of my life where ninety minutes could resolve my dramatic tension and produce a happy ending. Instead, I was to book a flight to Halifax where I would live with people who I did not know in a house run by nuns. My options were few. This was the only escape route, dressed up as nice, best and possible.

I sat alone in the examining room staring at the piece of paper in my hand. The answer. The solution. A plan. My doctor had said something about the many parents out there who desperately want children but could not have them on their own. Parents who were waiting for a girl like me to make a mistake so that they could adopt, is what she meant. There were parents lined up in a baby queue, smiling and waiting with open arms. I would deliver a child and place that child in the care of people I did not know. It was a lot to comprehend. It was a lot to bear. It was the path we chose.

Rob saw it as the best option. I would go away, have the baby and then return as if nothing had happened. No risk of his family or mine or our friends finding out. No local hospital to involve. It was a tidy, out of the way solution. Pack Mary up, put her on a plane and the nasty business of my pregnancy would be on its way to Halifax. We agreed, but I was the one who had to do it. On my own. He was not coming, nor would he visit.

I was the one carrying a child and that child was stirring emotions and love and connection I could not speak about. I was becoming its mother. My body, my mind and my heart were inextricably linked to the life growing into my reality and my forever. I did not speak of such things to Rob. I held them close to me. I shared them with the girl in my hallway mirror. I rolled around with them in my sleep and dreams. I worried over them on my commutes to and from work, when the heavy tug of my ever-increasing belly weighed on me physically and mentally.

I took the piece of paper my doctor gave me, folded it and pressed it inside my pocket. I walked out of her office, out of the building and out of myself.

I did what I told myself I had to do.

PART II

HALIFAX

she held it in
like breath
under water
sensing she could drown
the importance
of breathing evident
the need to exhale old
and take in new
still she held it in
unsure
when she could let it go
and return to the flow
of living

Sister M

I walked into the Halifax airport wearing a cotton summer dress and a winter coat, trying to conceal myself inside the unbuttoned flaps.

"Mary?" the woman in front of me said, more a statement than a question. She had come up from behind me as I pulled my suitcase from the luggage carousel, making me jump at the sound of her voice.

I searched the face of the short, serious woman in front of me, trying to figure out if she was the nun who was supposed to meet me.

"Sister M," she replied, reaching out to shake my hand. I took it, noting her firm grip around my small hand. She reached for my suitcase and led me toward the exit and out to the parking lot.

"How did you know me?" I asked.

"It must be one hundred degrees outside, and you are the only person in the whole place wearing a winter coat." And then after a slight pause, she leaned in and half whispered, "All the girls arrive wearing a coat."

As if that would make me feel better. How could I be like all the other girls? That was impossible.

Earlier that morning as I dressed for the airport, I'd convinced myself that the lightweight woollen coat looked proper for late summer. Standing sideways to look in my full-length mirror, I was sure it hid my swelling bulk. It was the most money I'd ever paid for a coat, but pre-pregnancy, it had fit me so perfectly and was so elegant that I'd splurged. Now it was my cloak of deception.

I saw instantly that Sr. M was blunt, candid and not to be fooled. She made me nervous. She saw through me, and it made me wonder how many others had done the same over the past few months. Like Walmart girl. Like the women in my office. Like the mother upstairs. Like my mirror that showed me every single day that I was not fooling anyone. I was pregnant. Plain and simple. Right there in my reflection. The bump of certainty that stuck out from my otherwise skinny frame.

As we emerged from the airport, I felt the sun's intensity. I hurried behind Sr. M as she strode through the rows of cars across the wide parking lot. I could smell the wool of my coat cooking in the hot sun, but I refused to take it off. We found her car, a rather proper Subaru station wagon. Sr. M heaved my suitcase into the back and stood with her hand outstretched for my coat. She raised her eyebrows and waited. I hesitated, then slipped it off and handed it to her. I looked around for anyone who might be watching. Sr. M rolled her eyes and let out a sigh, not the least bit perturbed that I was looking directly at her. She unlocked and opened the side door for me, and I slid into the front passenger seat. The oven inside the car made me grateful that I had removed my coat. Surely that was what Sr. M had been thinking. I said nothing. I was too anxious, being so close to someone I did not know and already sort of feared.

Sr. M was a short, stern woman from Boston. She was more practical than cordial, and it took some effort for her to smile and make conversation. Everything about her was short. Her hair, her body, her arms, her legs, her mannerisms. All short, quick and direct. While Sr. M had some of the characteristics of nuns I'd encountered in Newfoundland (serious and stern among them), she lacked the softness I was hoping to find in the Sisters of Charity, who ran the Home of the Guardian Angel. She spoke with a Boston accent, drawing out her a's, overruling the r's. It was an endearing quality that made me like her despite my discomfort. I figured that, because I was a girl in trouble and a Protestant, she probably assumed my soul was damned to hell anyway. I was an act of charity for her to store up good graces in heaven, while I was certainly doomed to the devil's underworld.

I had grown up being told by Catholic kids in my small town that I was a dirty Protestant and that only Catholics made it into heaven. By the time I was a teenager, my retort was that I would rather burn in hell with my fellow Protestants, having a party for eternity, than be in heaven with a bunch of stuck-up, snobby Catholics. It did not win me any new friends, but sniping back felt better than just taking the abuse. Of course, the Protestant crowd had their own issues. We hated back and were just as judgemental.

When I learned that the United Church of Canada did not want to ordain homosexuals, I knew my days of sitting in a pew were limited. I chose to believe in a God who accepts and loves everyone. It was a great irony that I was about to live in a home for unwed pregnant girls run by nuns.

I felt alone. Every girl I had seen that summer had a flat belly and a carefree attitude. Carefree had been swept away from me like clouds on a windy summer day. And here I was, bringing my rather twisted understanding of the Catholic religion along with my precarious situation into a setting for which I had no bearings and little preparation.

The sun beat in through the windshield, cheerfully mocking my worries. I was twenty-one years old. Old enough to keep my unborn child. Old enough to not need the father. But young enough, confused enough, that I was willing to harbour "our secret." I'd come to Halifax without a single member of my family knowing what was happening to me. Now it would be me, three Catholic nuns, and a group of young women who each came to this place with stories of shame, regret and indisputable bravery.

Sr. M pulled into the driveway of the imposing house that was to be my home for the coming weeks. It loomed above the drive and into the towering maple trees that surrounded it. It was a fairy-tale kind of house, alluring and mysterious, three stories with dormers along a peaked roof. At street level, the oversized front door at the top of wide stairs and flanked by tall windows gave it an air of aristocracy. It spoke to me of dinner parties, elegant guests arriving by horse and carriage for festivities and laughter. Evenings when the women swirled in taffeta skirts, bedecked with elaborate hairstyles, chattering and gossiping, while the men took their brandy in the drawing room, smoking pipes by the fire, speaking of business and politics. I imagined myself one of them for a moment, arriving through the door in a glamorous gown, linked arm in arm with my handsome beau, scandalously unmarried and haughtily in love with ourselves and life. I was indeed arriving scandalously, unwed, the beau nowhere to be seen. Instead, I entered with a short, stern nun—so much for haughty.

Sr. M opened the front door, motioning for me to go ahead as she wielded my suitcase and coat into the hallway. It took a moment for my eyes to adjust from the bright sunlight to the cool, shaded foyer. She laid the suitcase aside with my coat on top and pointed to a doorway on my right. Inside that room, I could hear the drone of an afternoon game show on television. Nervous, I stood still, not really wanting to meet anyone.

"Please, go in," she urged as she pushed me along with an impatient wave of her hand.

I hesitantly walked into the room. Couches, armchairs and rocking chairs were organized unevenly around the perimeter of the spacious sitting room. At the front, there was a wide window beside a round table and chairs. The television was perched on a shelf, high up on the wall, just to the right. Scattered around the room were several girls, all visibly pregnant. They sat with their bellies propped in front of them like tables; in fact, one girl ate from a plate balanced on her stomach. Another absentmindedly crocheted something atop her sizable pregnant mound. They were slouched and dazed in front of the television, for the most part oblivious to us. All but one of the girls looked younger than me.

Sr. M marched into the center of the room and stood squarely, hands on hips, between the girls and the television to capture their attention.

"This is the new girl. Mary." She pitched this announcement from deep in her chest as though weary of having done it many times before. Suddenly, all eyes were on me.

The new girl.

I was one of them. I was one of the pregnant girls now expected to assimilate and find her chair in this drab, depressing room. The thought made my heart sink. I don't recall if anyone said hello or introduced themselves because all I could focus on were the protests in my head at the idea of being one of these forlorn, knocked-up girls. I might be pregnant, I thought, but by God, I was not one of them. I was a university graduate with an honours degree, for God's sake! I felt separate from and better than those girls.

They eyed me warily. Perhaps they saw their own fear when they'd arrived. They took me in, looked me up and down, knowing that soon enough I would get past my pride just as they had. Soon enough I would find a seat along the wall and take afternoon naps on the couch right there with the rest of them. Soon enough I would be grateful for their presence and our shared companionship. Soon enough, I would be one of them.

The introduction over, Sr. M moved us on to the kitchen. It was spacious and open with a wide window at the back that looked out on lush greenery. The U-shape of the peach-coloured counter made an island through the middle, a clean and shiny blank space. The kitchen married homey and industrial in an odd relationship, as if someone could not decide which it should be.

Sr. M explained that Sr. G came every weekday morning to help us prepare the lunch and evening meals. Lunch was served promptly at noon. "Sr. G sets the menu and readies the food for the evening cooking; the girls do the cutting, dicing and slicing along with her. She leaves after that, and the girls do the final preparations, cooking and serving," she added, noting that Sr. G. was away on vacation but returning the following Monday. I got the impression that the kitchen was entirely this Sr. G's domain. As it was Saturday, I wondered what happened on weekends but did not dare ask. I assumed that Sr. G must have a plan for those days as well.

I followed Sr. M from the kitchen into a giant dining room. I was silently wondering if Sr. G would be like her, another earnest nun who fulfilled her role with frowning briskness. Would she shout orders and demand perfectly cut carrots and potatoes? Deny lunch to anyone who did not meet her standards? Perhaps she was the reason for the impeccable condition of the countertops. Another nun performing her duties of charity under the guise of godliness.

Sr. M breezed around the dining room explaining the process of serving, sharing and cleaning up after meals, as well as their timing. The long wooden dining room table was diagonally placed through the middle of the room. At the far end were two large rectangular windows that looked out upon maple trees. It looked as if a cafeteria table had been set up in an elegant dining space.

From the dining room, we entered a little hallway that led back to the front foyer. On the right was a tiny sitting room, with what appeared to be the original furniture from my imagined glory days of the house. Inside were two armchairs in paisley and a French sofa with curved, ornate wooden legs and spiral trim along the back. In the middle sat an oval coffee table, gleaming under the sunlight, not a speck of dust. The wallpaper and the art on the walls looked English countryside, like stepping into a Thomas Hardy novel. It made me want to curl up in one of the chairs with a book or my writing notepad. It was far more appealing than the wretched TV room across the hall. But

Sr. M was already explaining, quite firmly, that this room was only for receiving visitors; otherwise, it was off limits. I knew I would not be receiving visitors. I was disappointed. But I would come to pass by that room and see girls with their families sitting together in hushed, strained conversations and realize that the absence of visitors was not such a bad thing after all.

Sr. M closed the French door to the room with a decided thud to emphasize that she meant what she said. She brushed past me to pick up my suitcase and handed me my coat. With a nod, she instructed me to follow her up the stairs. I reached to take the suitcase, but she shook her head like this was another rule of the house—pregnant girls could not carry their own luggage. She steadied herself with a hand on the bannister as she prepared for the climb. I quietly ascended the stairs behind her as she strained for the breath to talk and lift my suitcase up each rise. She explained how many bedrooms were on the second floor, along with her private apartment. Coming to the top stair, she set the suitcase down with a great exhale. I sensed she was about to emphasize another important detail. She pointed to the door of her apartment and said that when she went in there, she expected complete quiet and privacy. She was not to be interrupted unless there was an emergency and that would most likely mean someone was in labour. Nor did she want to be bothered unless the labour was advancing, the girl was dilating, and the contractions were strong and evenly timed. She caught my horrified, open-mouth stare and halted her monologue to ask, "You have been taking prenatal classes, haven't you? You know about labour and ... Dear heaven, you have not been taking classes. Well, we will get that fixed. You can join prenatal classes at the Grace Maternity Hospital on Monday."

I knew virtually nothing about labour, contractions or what to expect. I had seen glimpses on television but had avoided reading about it. The pamphlets from Planned Parenthood sat unopened in my night table drawer at home. I had heard women talk about labour and it always sounded like a near-death experience. Dilating? What was dilating, I wondered. It sounded awful. I was twenty-one, and my sex education amounted to having had sex. I knew the sex part but not the part about delivering a baby. Well, I knew it had to come out and from where. But not until that moment had I spent any time thinking about the physical reality or the terminology of delivery. Sr. M's details unsettled me.

In the 1970s, sex education amounted to poor, made-for-middle-school films, one for boys and one for girls. There was no depiction of how the boy's body and the girl's body came together to kiss or, heaven forbid, have intercourse. There was no discussion of actual sex. That was left to be discovered in the back seat of a car with "Stairway to Heaven" playing on the radio. The teachers skirted the "don't have sex" portion of the curriculum in a general, "Please don't ask" way, and then, relieved, sent us back to our classrooms. Neither was sex discussed at home.

What I knew of labour and delivery was from scattered conversations, a couple of posters in my doctor's office and Hollywood. My mother had said once that you forgot about the pain when you had the baby in your arms. At the mention of pain, the conversation was over for me. I refused to go to a library to check out books on the subject. The internet would have been a great friend in those days. (As would readily available birth control, but abstinence was the proper Christian way.)

So, when Sr. M asked me about prenatal classes, I stood there help-less, unable to respond to the question. But she knew. I was sure it must be another standard mistake of the new girls, all part of our youth, in-eptitude and unwed shame.

What I came to learn about Sr. M, though, was that she was a practical woman who believed in being prepared. She sent the girls to prenatal classes because, when it was our time to deliver, we would be grateful we knew what the heck was happening and how to handle it.

Having had her brief rest, she reached down and reloaded my suit-case against her hip as she prepared to climb the next flight of stairs to the third floor. I followed along once more. Arriving on the top floor, Sr. M stopped in the hallway, deposited the suitcase with another re-sounding thump, and said, "You have a choice of rooms. There is this larger one to the right of the stairs." She opened the door. "It has two beds. You would be alone now, but as soon as another girl shows up, you will have to share."

I looked around the room. It was spacious and sunny. The furni-ture looked much like my university dorm room furnishings—twin beds, a couple of dressers. There were two windows with a rocking chair in front of one of them. It struck me as odd that a rocking chair, a mother and child sort of chair, would be here in a room for a girl who was not going to rock her baby. Sharing a room was not something I was interested in, though.

Seeing my reluctance, Sr. M went quickly on to say, as she exited the room and headed down the hall, "There is another room available, a single. It's small, but you would have it to yourself." She opened the door to the room at the end of the hall. It was tucked behind the stairs that came up through the center of the house. Inside was a single bed, a small white dresser and a little closet. The best part, the part that made it the room for me, was a triangular crawl space with a mattress and pillows, across from the bed, under the slanted roof. You had to bend down and enter on hands and knees, but once in, there was a dormer window with a lovely view out to the maple trees and the street below. It was a hideaway, a treehouse of sorts, the treehouse I had wanted as a little girl. A cozy corner just for me and my thoughts. I did not hesitate.

"This is the one I want."

Sr. M had been quietly watching me, perhaps knowing that this was the room I would choose. She smiled her earnest smile and went back into the hallway to get my suitcase and deposit it at its destination.

"Oh, and one more thing. There's a closet in the hallway. In it are maternity clothes. You are welcome to take whatever you need. Whatever fits. At the far end of the hall is the bathroom for this floor only."

She stood smiling at me, almost kindly, for a few brief seconds. Then just as quickly, the smile was gone, and her face resumed its sternness. She nodded and withdrew, leaving me alone to unpack and settle into my new space.

I was grateful for the solitude.

The first thing I did was crawl into the little, hidden space to look out the window. I stayed there for a long time. I was tired. I fell back into the pillows. I let myself cry. I felt I'd been stolen from my life in Newfoundland. It struck me hard that no family or friends knew where I was or what was to come. I was doing this alone. I was scared. So much of what was happening made me uncomfortable, but this little room at the top of an old house was a small sign of hope. It was my private retreat from everyone downstairs, from the Sisters of Charity, from whatever lay ahead. I did not know how I would make it, but I knew I had to stay where I was and find a way through until my baby was born.

My conversation with Sr. M made me acutely apprehensive about labour and delivery because until she spoke about it, I had been able to avoid thinking about the inevitable. Getting to Halifax had been enough to handle, but now the reality of why I was there demanded acknowledgement. I was going to have a baby. That baby was going to come out of my body through my vagina. As I looked down at myself, I wondered if I was equipped to handle birth. What if I was not, and the doctors had to cut the baby out of me? I pushed that thought away as quickly as it came.

I retrieved my Discman from my purse and placed it on the windowsill for later. I crawled out from my hideaway and sat on the narrow single bed to unpack my clothes. I put what little I had in the dresser and closet and slid the suitcase under the bed. For now, this was my space and privacy. Over time, I came to feel safe in that room. There has never been a room before or since that meant more to me. It taught me that space can become a reflection of who I am and what I need. It was comfort and repose in an unsettled reality.

Over the years I have recalled that room and revisited its memories. Each time, I am curled up with a blanket and pillow looking out the dormer window. Sometimes I imagine looking in the window from outside to see myself as I was then. I see a small person with a swelling belly. I want to reach in and take my younger self in my arms. I want to console her, sing to her, and let her rest her head on my older, wiser self.

I want to assure her that, one day, it will be okay.

I like to think that those who came to live in that room afterward sensed me there, that in the dark of a tearful night my sense of hope might have emerged for them. That they too crawled into the secret hideaway and watched the birds in the trees. And like me, they might have watched the green August leaves turn to autumn marigold and auburn and glorious red. In the weeks that unfolded, I needed that safe nest, a place of my own within the struggles and fears I shared with the girls downstairs.

you are not alone
in your fears
I feel them too
like you
with you
we might conquer
them together
with shreds
of courage
torn from
the cloth
of desire
that we light on fire
with the belief
that nothing
can stop us
but us

sisterhood

My things unpacked, I prepared to go back downstairs. Now that the guided tour was over, I had to face the others on my own. It was late afternoon and the house seemed asleep. Maybe everyone was napping, I thought. I leaned over the railing. No movement. No sounds. I was thirsty and a little hungry. I had not eaten since breakfast and hadn't had anything to drink on the plane to avoid walking up the aisle to the bathroom.

I walked stealthily along the hallway and slipped into the bathroom to look at myself before going downstairs, closing the door and peering into the mirror. I looked tired. I was tired. I splashed cool water on my face several times, letting it drip from my chin and fingertips. I patted my face dry with a towel and tugged my curls into haphazard order.

How did I get here of all places? I should know have known better. I should have done better.

I stood there for a few moments fighting back tears and feeling sorry for myself. No amount of praying to Jesus had saved me. I was here living out my fate. I heaved a heavy sigh and opened the bathroom door to go face that dismal sitting room and my new companions. I felt a little more open to meeting the girls that I had earlier dismissed as being nothing like me. They were like me. I was like them. That was why I had come to this place.

The sitting room situation was much like I had left it. The television was still on, the girls scattered about the room sleepily and passively engaged in some daytime soap opera. One girl, tall, blond and very pregnant, sat at the table by the window making something. As I drew closer, I could see that it was jewelry, striking pieces made from gathered stones and twisted wires. She looked up, smiling, and then spread her hands over the top of her ample belly as she smoothed the fabric of her dress down, lovingly and proudly emphasizing her shape. It was a habit that she repeated for as long as I knew her. A sort of adoration for and admission of her pregnant form, voluptuous and Rubenesque.

"I like your jewelry," I told her in a cautious attempt to be friendly.

She said thanks and kept on working. I felt she wanted to talk but, like me, she didn't know what to say. I sat at the table to watch her. She carried on for a few minutes until one of the other girls said that it was time to prepare dinner. Several of them got up to go to the kitchen, including the girl at the table. I stood as well and asked if I could help. I was told by the girl who seemed to be in charge that I would be put on the schedule. I followed them into the kitchen anyway. The schedule was on the wall, showing a list of names and kitchen duties spread equitably out over the week.

"Sr. G will put you on there when she gets here on Monday."

This came from the girl in charge, who was short, muscular and wore her belly like a watermelon. She reminded me of girls from around the bay in Newfoundland. Tough. Straightforward. Ready for a fight and easily able to take anyone on, no matter their size. She could hit you hard with just her glare. She moved quickly across the kitchen, focused on her tasks, seeming eager to complete them. She still wore regular street clothes, jeans and a plaid shirt. Her pregnancy seemed in odd juxtaposition to her nature. She was hard, with an edge. I wondered if I were to dare to mention her pregnancy, she might fight me and make me take it back. I tried to imagine what kind of boy would have been with her. I flashed on violence and rough sex in an alley. No kissing. No tenderness. Just raw sex. All this was going through my head when I realized she was standing in the middle of the kitchen waiting for me to answer a question I had missed.

"Where are you from?"

"Newfoundland," I sputtered.

She considered that with a slight tilt of her head. For a split second, I saw a softness come across her face. A tiny wrinkle at the corner of her eyes and a pursing of her lips made her seem normal, possibly even kind. She said she was from Cape Breton, which made me believe she appreciated me being a Newfoundlander. We shared similar cultures, music, storytelling and family traditions. Her shy smile made me like her. It made me hope that the boy had been passionate. That he had kissed her sweetly. We would never be friends, she and I, but my heart held a spot for her from that moment on. It was not something I could tell her. She was one of those mean girls in high school who spat on the ground, smoked on the steps at recess and said "fuck it" all the time. You could never be her friend, but you sure as hell did not want to be her enemy.

"Newfoundland? Never been there. But I hear it's nice."

It was the point in a conversation where the person might ask more questions about the place you come from. But she just moved on, taking out pots and turning on the stove. No one else asked either. I was to learn that, in a situation like the one we were in—a situation like a house for unwed mothers where everyone had come to have babies they do not plan to keep—the less said, the better. This was not a Girl Scout camp. This was not a retreat. And it was certainly not a vacation. This was the hard stuff of life. This was a house where girls, young women from various backgrounds, were suddenly in proximity. And the only thing we really shared was our blighted circumstances. There would be no pajama parties where we giggled and talked until the sun came up. There would be no sharing of secrets, except the secret we held against the forces of those we left behind. We were in this march together for as long as it took and then we would part ways and carry on. No letters or Christmas cards with photos tucked inside. No reunions. No sorority.

The greatest incongruity for me was that this hard girl with the fierce facade was the one who, out of all of us, kept her baby in the end. One evening after I returned to the house following the birth of my son, Sr. M stood in the hallway outside my bedroom door to tell me how the girl from Cape Breton had returned to claim her daughter. She had gone home after delivery and was supposed to come back to sign the adoption papers. Instead, she asked for her daughter. And kept her. Sr. M said they were as poor as church mice and the baby had a bleak future, but the girl took her baby anyway.

"There is no telling why. She just said it was her baby and that was that," Sr. M said, looking bewildered.

It was her baby. And perhaps the future was bleak. Perhaps that child was bound to grow up and be like her mother, hardened and callused. But perhaps, and this is the eternal optimist in me, perhaps that baby girl changed everything. Through love and joy and blessings. Perhaps that mother needed the love her baby girl brought with her. It may have been the first sign of love, the longed-for pure love, that transformed and saved her.

I could write this story in multiple ways, but each version would only be imaginings. The truth, though, is that I admired her then, and still, for having the backbone to return to the Home and take her daughter home to raise her. What I wished I had done, she did. It was the kind of strength I had considered—but I chose another.

she was
grace
amazing
light
shining
in the gloom
of a room
that waited
for her
to arrive

Sr. G

On Monday morning at breakfast, Sr. M reminded us that Sr. G would soon be back. I sat chewing my toast, wondering what this new nun would bring to our motley conglomeration. My imagination painted her as the kitchen tyrant, barking orders while she used Bible quotes to reinforce the evidence of our sins and reckless pasts. I thought she might come through the door and line us up against the wall so she could inspect us before making us peel, cut and prepare the two remaining meals of the day. I imagined her stout and dressed all in black with a habit. I imagined her crossing herself every time she saw a pregnant belly. I was imagining such ridiculous things when I looked up and there she was.

Sr. G was nothing like I had imagined. To best describe my reaction, I must simply say that an angel walked into my life that day. I will never forget that first sight of her, and I have never lost how she made me feel. Sr. G was of average height with wavy, greying hair. She had a softness, a happy plumpness around the middle, that made her lovely. She wore a blue flowered dress that morning with practical, brown shoes, possibly Hush Puppies. Her face was kind and sweet, gently wrinkled from years of smiling upon everyone she met. Her eyes were happy and fell upon me with joyful expectation. I did not know her age, but I would guess that at the time she was in her early sixties. She walked into the kitchen a quiet, gentle force that changed the energy in the room. Even Sr. M smiled and greeted Sr. G with a graciousness that let me see she admired and respected this woman.

When Sr. G saw me, she came to meet me, asked my name and called me "Mary dear," making me love her instantly. I lost myself in the folds of her arms as she hugged me that first time. She was sweetness and calm. She was love personified. She was the best version a nun could be if you wrote her as a character in a novel.

Love showed up in the darkest times of my life. It found me, sought me out, so I could survive despite my doubts and fears. That's what Sr. G was to me. She was the love that showed up and saved me over and over while I shared time with her in that house. Her warmth wrapped around me and offered me a gentle place to lean into during the two months that I knew her in Halifax. She was the kind of nun that allowed me to see that God, whatever form God takes, is real.

I met Sr. G over thirty-five years ago. Yet putting her name on the page reminds me that I have never lost sight of her peaceful expression. I raced back from prenatal classes and hospital appointments to be sure I would have time with her before she left each day. I helped her prepare food in the kitchen just to talk with her and be in her presence. She always had time for me. I was certain she looked forward to seeing me too. I don't remember specifically what we talked about, but to quote Maya Angelou, "people will never forget how you made them feel." Sr. G made me feel loved, she made me feel special—she made me feel normal in my most abnormal of days.

When I left Newfoundland, I thought about my mother and how sad she would have been that I was going away to have a baby all on my own. My mother would have wanted me to come home to have and keep the baby. There were moments when the thought of my mother's love and support almost broke me. I wanted her to take me in and tell me everything would be all right. My mother's face haunted me. I longed for her comfort, and the need left me bereft. Often, when I retreated from the others in the house to my bedroom alcove to be alone, it was my mother who came to mind.

Sr. G reminded me of my mom as she bustled about the kitchen, humming and lovingly preparing food with us. My mother's kitchen was the heart and soul of our home. There was always food being prepared. Berry pies. Golden crusty loaves of bread. Soups. Stews. As she moved through the kitchen, Sr. G. assuaged my deep longing for my mother. She did not look like my mother, nor was she her replacement, but without her I would not have coped as well as I did.

I never once felt shame or embarrassment with Sr. G. She accepted me without judgement, and she honoured the fact that a child was growing inside me. She encouraged me to see that bringing a life into the world is a magnificent miracle. After knowing me for a few weeks, she told me I was blossoming. She remarked that I was no longer the scared, skinny girl she had seen on that first morning. She reminded me that it was important to take care of myself so that both the baby and I would be healthy.

She did not quote scripture or preach to me about salvation or my lack of eternal worth. In fact, I do not remember her mentioning God at all. She was just a good person. She was generous and kind, and funny too. We often laughed together as we stood side by side chopping and slicing vegetables. A lot can be said over such work in the kitchen, in the harmony of hands and hearts and food.

I wish my mom could have met Sr. G. I felt that the two of them would have put on the teakettle and settled into a conversation like old friends. It would have been good for my mother to see that this woman took care of me when I needed it most, and it would have amazed her that it was a Catholic nun who brought me such comfort. I wonder now if my mother would have understood me better if she had seen me through the eyes of Sr. G, who cared for me without judgement. In her presence, I felt whole. When I was with her, I was happy. Sr. G called forth the true me, the one that yearned for creativity and dreamed of a future.

She would let me talk while she listened, laughing at the funny things I said. She saw me, really saw me, and that made all the difference. She said she wondered what the future would be for me and what I might become. She encouraged me to believe that my life would be remarkable. That I was already that and more. I needed these conversations. Shame can place a powerful grip on confidence and self-image. It can shatter and destroy you. But hope overrules shame.

Sr. G was sweet and reassuring. She liked me, and I knew it. I liked me too when I was with her.

In those times, pregnancy stayed out of mind, even if not out of view. I am not sure how Sr. G enabled this, but it was an essential part of coping. It was an escape, a way out of my state of mind where I could be someone other than the pregnant failure living in a home for unwed mothers. I needed that salve on my wounded pride. I needed that care to allow me to feel something other than shame and worry.

Sr. G told me greatness was in my future and that she could not wait to hear about it. It was the kind of message that I could get lost in. I dared to believe her. I trusted that she had a direct link to God, so it made sense to trust whatever she said. It was the kind of message I wished I had heard all those Sundays in church instead of threats of damnation. Throughout my life, I have never met another person who better embodied God and love than Sr. G. When she laid her hand on mine and spoke to me, I could believe that God was in her touch. She was what I felt religion ought to be. Love and kindness. No judgement. No threats. And no mention that only Catholics go to heaven.

Sr. G showed me that heaven is not a destination in the sky where we go when we die. Heaven is the place within us where we are our best selves, our most open and honest. There will be no cloud that ascends upward with the chosen few on board. There is no hell below for the millions outside the chosen faith to sink down to, wretched for eternity. I have seen enough of hell on earth to know that it's right here. Our direction is set not by sinful transgressions but by how we see ourselves, by how we choose to live and especially by how we treat others. I am inclined towards heaven, especially the kind of heaven Sr. G unveiled. I am grateful for her lessons and the light she shone into my darkness.

she wore
a red dress
out of place
she seemed
as though
she walked in
to someone else's
dream
and the sight
of her
changed everything
into a hue
of scarlet
possibilities
quickening
the pulse
of those who
saw her

Sr. R

The third nun was Sr. R, our counsellor. Counselling was not something I had ever experienced, but I soon looked forward to it each week as it gave me someone to talk to, someone that listened. The first I heard of Sr. R was that she was arriving back from vacation in the Bahamas. She sounded extraordinary for that reason alone.

I was sitting in the TV room when she came through the front door. I felt her, took in her energy, even before I saw her. It was as though a fresh wind swept into the room in front of her, heralding her unique presence. When I looked up, I saw an aura around this lovely woman. She was light and beauty and grace. She wore a white, flared dress with bright red and yellow flowers, a red belt cinching her waist. Her hair was a glamourous ginger, cut in a short, modern style, and her faced glowed with a new tan, making her freckles bright and pretty. She sparkled and glistened in the dull light of the sitting room. She literally swirled into the room, smelling of powder and sunshine. But it was her smile and the way her eyes danced that made her truly lovely. She looked into my eyes with such warmth that I could not look away.

Sr. R made being a nun seem like a desirable vocation. She exuded joy. I have heard it said that there are people in the world, like Mother Teresa, in whose eyes you see the face of God looking back at you. That was Sr. R. I liked her instantly. She went against everything I knew about the Catholic faith. She was happy and carefree. Nothing about her was stern or scolding. From the first moment, I wanted to be near her. Life improved just by standing in her vicinity. Worry was replaced by her optimism and positivity. I did not know a nun could be so pretty, so engaging and so alive. It was compelling!

Being with her made me think about my years of church, when as a young girl, my parents gave me no choice about attending. I could not tell them, but church made me feel like an outsider who did not have the code to be let into the experience. I watched my father pray and wondered what he said as he leaned forward on bended knee, hand on the pew in front of him, his head on his hand. I watched him from the corner of my eye, not wanting him to find me gawking when he was done. I admired his dedication and open display of ritual and was grateful that he never suggested that I do as he did. I found it challenging to keep my eyes closed during the Lord's Prayer, and worried that other people would open their eyes and catch me watching them.

It was Sr. R. who helped me make sense of what it can look like to believe in God without participating in congregational requirements. God, it seemed, can be accessed anywhere. Belief can be a beautiful expression of yourself that you share with others. Belief from within—a sparkle in your eyes that says life is good and to be celebrated.

During our appointments, Sr. R was patient, gently drawing what I wanted and needed to say from me. Her office was bright and cheerful, like her. The August sun came in the window as we sat together. I relaxed and became open. She asked questions that went into the hidden, unexplored parts of my situation. She spoke with candour and care. I did not realize how restorative it could be to tell someone my fears or how close to the surface my repressed emotions were. Sr. R provided a safe place where I could examine them with validation and guidance, and without worrying about being labelled a bad person.

We began with me rambling on about everything but pregnancy. I told her about my family and the parts of my life that made me proud. She enjoyed my offbeat sense of humour, my Newfoundland way of making fun of myself. I told her about leaving my small town to attend university. How my parents drove me to the city in my dad's pickup with my suitcases and boxes tied down in the back, making me think we looked like the *Beverly Hillbillies*. How, when I registered for my classes, my dad walked with me to write the cheque to pay my tuition. And how my mother made up my bed with the quilt she had made for me, helped me put away my clothes in the small closet and then walked out of my room, leaning on my dad's arm as she began to cry tears that continued for the whole trip back home. How we were small town people with big hearts—saying that, I got emotional because I was so far from them.

Then slowly, I told her how I had gotten pregnant. I told her about Rob. I told her about our visit to Planned Parenthood, and how having the baby was the only option, but it had to be verified for him. I hesitated to tell her how he had pressed for an abortion even though he'd heard it was unsafe, but then told her anyway. She listened patiently as I painted a rehearsed, optimistic picture of the plan Rob and I had constructed and agreed upon. My earnest desire was to appear competent and intelligent.

Somewhere in the middle of my speech, she held up her hand and stopped me.

"Are you sure you want to give up your child up for adoption? Is this his plan? Are you certain?"

"Yes," I responded in a squeaky, small voice.

I babbled on. I told her how we had just graduated from university. I told her we were too young, unprepared for a child. I wanted the child to have two parents, a good home, financial security. The list of justifications kept coming, stirred up from the long days and nights of convincing myself that this was for the best. That he wanted it and I wanted it. That there was a "we" in the plan.

She watched me silently, studying my face more than my words.

"You are not there yet. But we have time. You need to be sure."

"Oh, I am sure," I replied. "I mean, I have to ..."

She smiled at me and said that she wanted me to think about it. She wanted me to forget what he wanted and focus on what I wanted. It was obvious that he was nowhere in sight. There was only me in the room.

"Giving up a child is too important to not be sure," she cautioned. We would talk more at our next session. I was baffled by her adamant request. It rattled me. Yet, I had been struggling with that very question.

Was I sure?

I lay in bed that night reviewing our conversation and the way Sr. R had looked at me, her patient but firm expression resolutely requiring me to do more work on my decision. There are women whose experience in a home for unwed mothers was radically different than mine, who report that nuns gleefully took children from them and profited from the adoptions. I am not certain of the financial gains of the Home of the Guardian Angel, but Sr. R did not press me towards adoption. Rather, she counselled me to know within myself if it was right. She emphasized that even after my child was born, I would have two weeks, required by law in Nova Scotia as a waiting period, to change my mind. Up until the moment I signed the adoption papers, my child would be mine to keep if I chose.

During our subsequent sessions, Sr. R and I went into the uncharted territory of my heart. She asked me questions that I had not dared ask myself up until then. She explored the gravity of the choice to be made. She held up a different kind of mirror for me to look in and see myself, a mirror that was less about reflection and more about discovery. Seeing who I was far beneath the surface. I was a young woman trying to comprehend and deal with the serious situation I was in and the serious choice I was to make for my life and the life of my unborn son.

I cried angry tears. I got mad. I hated Rob for letting me go to Halifax alone while his life carried on. I said that out loud to Sr. R and saw it as something I would forever hold against him, a resentment I added to the growing stack. I left Newfoundland with a plan to protect a secret between us when what I really wanted and needed was a shoulder to lean on. I needed him to share with me the strain and hurt that was as tangible as my growing fetus.

Choice. A small word that bears so much power. It was mine to make. When Sr. R got me to this juncture of understanding, I felt both free and trapped. I held jurisdiction over my future and that of my unborn child. I could discount what Rob wanted and go it alone in a new way. My way. When the day came to sign the adoption papers, it would be my name, my signature, on the dotted line. Not his. I had left Newfoundland with a joint plan, but now I was preparing to give up my child alone.

I considered keeping my son. In my private deliberations, it was there as a desirable possibility. I felt him alive within me, and I loved him. I wanted him. I realized that while I had not wanted to be pregnant, I did want my child. Hiding the pregnancy was about embarrassment, shame and saving face. But in the Home, away from everyone I knew, away from Rob, I could be openly pregnant. I enjoyed the changes in my body as it grew and bloomed in the open. I carried a child. A child that I loved.

In the weeks I spent with Sr. R, she led me into and through the wilderness of my heartache. She pushed me to feel, not just think, and then to consider those feelings as I sought to decide my fate and that of my unborn baby.

Ultimately, I chose adoption. I did it because I placed his life, his happiness, above my own. I knew I faced raising him as a single mother. Rob had been clear. Was I afraid of raising the baby alone, having to depend on my family, of moving back home? Yes. I was afraid of a lot of things, things that I did not want to be a part of my child's life.

At the time, I considered my life too. It would be a lie to say that what I did was a completely selfless act. I considered what it would mean to my carefully constructed reputation as the smart girl.

What remains, though, is my belief that I made the intelligent choice. As much as Sr. R urged me to consider my emotions, I was not emotionally mature enough to comprehend the gravity of my choice. I could justify it as an astute choice because, on my child's side, the advantages seemed overwhelming. On my side, it was about protection, reputation and the ability to start my adult life. Being a single parent was not part of that plan, and it seemed a huge disadvantage for both my child and me. Especially when the alternative was a prosperous couple who had checked all the parental boxes for a happy, healthy, loving home.

I am troubled
by silences
things not said
because
we are afraid
or ashamed
or both
silences
that take
personal power
dignity
our right to be
happy
silences need
to be broken
wide open
so we
can give up
hiding
and
hoping
and
change

larch street

The Home sat at the intersection of Coburg Road and Larch, a tree-lined street of large gracious homes framed by wide lawns and abundant flower gardens. It was easy to imagine living in one of those houses, on the kind of street where I supposed people had happy, safe lives. Lives without struggle. Moms and dads and kids sharing long summer days, autumn leaves, Thanksgiving dinners, Christmas mornings, snowfalls, spring rains, birthdays, graduations, weddings. The ideal.

I looked down at the round bulge of my belly. This child deserved all of that, a life that seemed far from my reach at twenty-one. As I looked out onto Larch Street from the dining room window, adoption seemed the right choice. I wanted that life for him. I could see it clearly. My little boy, climbing the steps to his house after jumping gleefully from the yellow school bus that delivered him home. The door would open, and there would be his mom, arms wide open to hug him home. Down the hall, there is a big wooden table with warm cookies and a tall glass of milk, waiting to be enjoyed over the day's stories of friends, recess and teachers. She would listen with her whole self to every word he said because he was the center of her world. She would love him like that because he was all she had ever dreamed of when she imagined a child to call her own. I let my mind wander daringly into this dream for my son despite the fact it strangled my heart knowing I would not be that mom.

It was if I was watching a movie of his life. I was not in the movie, not yet, but I was the producer, director and writer. It was my story for my son. I was willing it into place. Later in the movie, I could write myself into the script. I could have him search for and find me, or I could find him. Either way, we would be reunited. I might walk up the steps of his house, and he would open the door. He would know me instantly because we would look alike. The same wild curls. Same brown eyes. Same instant smile. It would be the made-for-television ending where you can't help but feel good while you cry and reach for tissues. I would wrap him in my arms and let the love that possessed me from the moment I conceived him pour out in my touch. And he would be back in my life forever.

"Cut! Take five. Everyone off the set!"

My mind was way ahead of reality, and it hurt. It hurt too much.

I turned away from the window. In here were pregnant girls from various parts of the Maritimes. Did the fathers at home struggle with their own guilt and shame? Did they know they were about to be fathers? If so, did they tell themselves she should have been more careful?

Whatever was happening back at home, we were here on our own. And when we gathered around the dining room table, it was much more than an act of sharing food and conversation. It was an unspoken connection, a time of bonding through common circumstances and limited choice while we passed the salt and pepper and obediently bowed our heads to say the blessing with Sr. M. It was an unspoken knowing that drew us one to another.

Larch Street. I too would one day be the mom with the husband, kids and house in suburbia. Yet I would never find the happy ever after, the fairy tale, the ideal version of a love story, no matter the square footage of the house or the calibre of cars in the driveway.

If I had known then that the house and address were meaningless in comparison to love, I would not have imagined my son happier in that life than with me. I was too inexperienced to see that love was the only thing that mattered. Love can make any place the best place to raise a child.

During my days at the Home, I became adept at reading faces and body language. The subtle sigh from the breast of a young woman lost in thought made me instinctively reach out my hand to acknowledge her. She would look up and into my eyes. She knew, and I knew, what was underneath that sigh. No words were required to convey the weight on her heavy heart. In those moments we saw that remaining pregnant was easier. While the baby remained inside, we remained mothers. No adoption to decide upon. No broken heart when it was done. No words can express how you feel when you know what is to come but don't know how you will survive it. So, when we saw the look or felt the pain in another person, we just reached out and held on until we both found the strength to move on. Until the next time.

Those young pregnant women changed me. Not much at first, but more as I matured into life. The odds of getting pregnant in the early

1980s were high and it was still considered to be the worst thing that could happen to a girl. In the company of these young women, I experienced my first real connection to the human experience and its many flaws and consequences. I was nothing like them, and yet we were entirely the same. We were the outcomes of choices, limitations and societal judgements. We suffered the same sadness, endured the same rejections, and ultimately faced the same choice—to place for adoption or keep the child we would deliver, essentially alone, in a strange place.

When I set out for Halifax, it seemed the worst thing in the world that I would live in a home for unwed mothers. I wanted to pull my cloak of shame over my head and hide inside. It was a cruel, heartless God who would leave my prayers unanswered and let me end up in such a place. But what seemed like the worst thing in the world turned out to be good. I see now I just needed to be patient and wait. All my tearful pleas and prayers were unnecessary. I was taken far out of my comfort zone and brought to an entirely unfamiliar place to learn life lessons that continue to influence my character even now.

Like Alice in Wonderland, I stepped through the looking glass to find myself in a most unexpected place. I was scared. I was lonely. I was shaken. But I was freed from everyone and everything connected to the past. The eclectic group of women who surrounded me provided a realization. I had not always been a kind sister to women along the way. But as I have grown into my own womanhood, I've lived steadfastly by the principle that it is part of my purpose to uplift other women, to celebrate our unique stories and struggles, and to never, ever let an opportunity to help pass me by.

Those young women, semi-outcasts, taught me to look beyond the obvious to find the real. The tragedy of the circumstances that brought us together gave rise to grit and tenacity. Memory has a way of reshaping when reflection and understanding are layered over the past. We see what happened with different eyes as we grow wiser; our judgements are replaced with understanding. I would be gentler with those women if I could go back and relive that time. But since that is not possible, I honour them by acknowledging what it took to live in the house on Coburg and Larch while we waited for the end and the beginning.

she is not about
to tell you
her secret
she will leave you
guessing
because
her intrigue
is the mystery
she will not
divulge
since it might
shatter
what matters
in her facade

prenatal party

Imagine a dull green room in the basement of a hospital. A bank of windows at the back are shuttered by shades that seem to shut out the light and hold in the grim. In the middle are a circle of uncomfortable chairs with scratchy brown cushions and one straight bar of wood that hits your back right below the shoulder blades. Posters on the walls, curled and torn at the corners, depict the various stages of pregnancy, from conception to birth.

Into that room comes a group of young pregnant girls, not at all eager for prenatal class.

Birth. The poster was in colour, showing the head of the baby emerging into a doctor's cradling hands. The baby in the picture looked peaceful, as though sleeping. I could not take my eyes away. Clarity hit me hard. In a few short weeks, a baby would emerge from my body. A living, breathing little human with a soul and a face that would reflect my own. Most of the time, I could walk around not acknowledging that birth and a child were imminent. As pregnant as I was, I went through the days not letting it intrude upon my thoughts. It was the way I got by.

The prenatal instructor walked into the room and took a seat in the circle. We all looked at her, waiting, while she clutched her clipboard to her chest and surveyed us. She smiled with a nervous earnestness suggesting that she braced herself for these classes. Young and plain, with hair in a neat ponytail, I guessed that this was probably her first real job. She would do this stint for as long as it took her to get something better.

She was probably grateful to not be one of us, I thought. No men here. No hopeful husbands eager to help their wives deliver their child. I imagined her later with friends at a local bar, her hair let loose, drinking cheap beer and laughing about the unfortunate pregnant lot she had suffered again today.

"Good morning," she now offered a little too brightly.

Mutters of good morning in response.

"Welcome to prenatal class!" She said this as though we had won a prize.

No response.

"Is this everyone's first time here?"

Was she fucking kidding? Quizzical looks.

I was sulky and already annoyed. I envied her job and career. I wanted to pull aside this girl who was likely my age and say, "Listen, I know this looks bad, but I am actually not the person you think I am. I just graduated from university. I have an English honours degree. This is simply an unfortunate sideline to my otherwise stellar life."

I needed humility but was trapped in arrogance.

She smiled weakly when no one responded and moved on. I wondered if this naive young woman knew that we would be going through labour with a nun at our side, not a husband or boyfriend or anyone else who knew and loved us.

As the classes progressed, our young instructor would catch herself referring to our "partner's role" and blush as she corrected herself. I felt for her, yet I enjoyed her discomfort too. I wanted her to be embarrassed and flustered. It was the only vestige of power I had, given my circumstances. Get it wrong, I thought. Say the wrong things. Apologize profusely while I sit here watching you squirm in your lack of understanding and compassion for me. Get the job done so you can retreat to your office, coffee and paperwork. Don't even dare to try and understand me. Because no matter what you think, you don't have a clue who I am.

That's what I thought. I could not help myself because sometimes feeling superior gave me a rush, like a drug, that temporarily relieved my queasy, sick feelings of doom.

I could tell that prenatal classes were designed for couples preparing together for the birth of their child. The birth of my son would not be a joint activity. I would not need sympathy breathing and pushing. I could not see Sr. M offering such support. What I needed was someone to step in and take my place, get this thing done for me. But since that was not going to happen, my best bet was to focus on my needs, my body, and the pain that would be mine to endure. Now that I was in a prenatal class, I could see that pain was a definite, something I had to prepare for and learn to manage.

I settled into prenatal classes with a combination of curiosity and alarm. I wanted to be prepared, but I also wished to be the girl who took off at the break and didn't come back. I felt uneasy with breathing techniques. I worried that I might hyperventilate. I decided that I could wing it. How hard could it be to breathe? I worried that I would somehow screw up. I certainly did not want a caesarean, a permanent scar on my body to conceal, forever worried that the mark would betray my secret. No, I decided then and there that I would deliver the baby the good old-fashioned way. My mother, slight of hip and small of frame, had delivered six kids without one caesarean. I chose to bet on having her genes, physical attributes and birthing prowess.

When class ended, we walked back to the Home, a ragged ensemble of bellies swaying inside loose coats. The first hint of fall tinged the late August air with a fresh coolness. University taught me that discussion gels knowledge, but this was not a situation where post-class conversation occurred. We held in our thoughts along with our fears. We were not heading for any kind of certification or graduation. The way forward was what we worried most about, and since there was no postnatal class for mothers who gave up their babies, we sucked that worry down inside.

When we passed store windows, I caught sight of our reflections. We looked like school girls on a field trip until you noticed our bulges. It surprised me to see myself like that. One of a group, sauntering along in the midday sunshine, my reflection an affirmation that I was indeed in a strange place, with strangers, enduring a strange time. Under different circumstances, I would have preferred to walk alone, but now I found some comfort within the group. Not one, but one of, surrounded by others who helped conceal me. Not that there was anyone that I knew in Halifax, but the worry never left me.

Like much of my stay in Halifax, prenatal classes were a paradox. Real but not real. They were something I did, but they were not me. I held myself aloof as if, through indifference, I might somehow rise above my circumstances. I went through the motions, I attended the classes, I walked with the other girls to and from, but I did not feel as if I was there. It might have been a coping mechanism, inserting distance between me and what I couldn't bear. I could laugh cruelly at my instructor because it provided some relief when nothing, not a damn thing, was funny.

*the first time
I was pregnant
he was in a rage
his fist
in my stomach
thought I would faint
wished I had
he owned me
from then on
because
I let him do it
again
and again
until I was numb
the first time
every time
any time
a little part of me
died inside
if only I could
go back
to the first time
I'd walk away
not looking back
and be free*

closet conversation

There was a small hallway closet on the second floor, converted into a makeshift phone booth for us to make collect calls. In the corner was an old wooden kitchen chair, on the wall a black rotary dial phone and, on the floor, toppling stacks of tattered phone books. I propped my feet on the phonebooks as I slouched in the chair, trying to find a comfortable position.

The old phonebooks smelled dusty and dank like they had been there for years. The wooden chair creaked under my weight, and I worried that the legs might snap, leaving me trapped in the corner under musty phonebooks and splintered wood. I wrapped the tangled phone cord in and out of my fingers when I was on a call. Someone had removed the closet door, possibly to make the space more accessible and less claustrophobic, but it made the tiny room open to those passing up and down the stairs too.

I only ever called one person, Rob. Since he was the only one who knew where I was and what was happening to me, he was the only person I could talk to during that time. I called my parents once, on my birthday, a carefully rehearsed conversation kept brief to avoid any unwanted questions. Rob and I spoke about once a week.

One telephone conversation remains with me above the rest—the one in which I asked him, "What if I keep the baby?"

He exploded. He got even angrier when I said that it was up to me. I let him shout and rant. I enjoyed the power I had being away from him. I knew that if I wanted to, I could keep my child and there was not a damn thing he could do about it. He knew it too, and it unnerved him. What I didn't know and would only find out on my first night back in Newfoundland was that his sister had gone through a secret pregnancy and delivered a baby while I was in Halifax. Despite their father's advice, she kept her daughter. This must have caused Rob to worry that I might do the same. It also meant he knew it was up to me.

After my return, I saw what keeping the baby would have meant for Rob—exclusion from his family, along with shame. His sister had been essentially disowned. The family denied the child to the point I once heard his mother exclaim to someone at a Mother's Day brunch that she was not yet a grandmother. Her nervous laugh contradicted her, but she held fast to her assertion. Rob and I were welcome in his family only because our child, the problem and the shame, was out of sight.

Family dynamics are a study in human behaviour. Why we do things is entrenched in norms and expectations that we are taught from childhood. We can be ruled by such matters to the point of not questioning them even when what we want and what we need are denied. We can put family above our own best interests to save face, retain favour and keep the peace. When I knew what Rob had seen his sister endure, it gave me perspective on what motivated him to shout me down when I mentioned keeping our baby. It seemed to me that he was so in need of his family's approval that he had to convince me to give up our child at any cost. His choice was more for his family than it was for him.

That night in the phone closet redefined us. I discovered I had a backbone. I knew by the end of that call that placing my son for adoption was my choice, mine alone, to make. It scared Rob, and I liked it.

I leaned back in the chair and let his anger spill out as I held the receiver away from my ear. I looked at the phone and smiled a little sanctimonious smirk. Despite being afraid of him, I was aware that he was far enough away I could just hang up. He repeatedly demanded that I confirm I would go through with the adoption. I let him squirm. In the end, I said that was still the plan, even though I hadn't truly decided. I just needed to end the call.

When we hung up, I climbed the stairs back to my room and lay on my bed thinking over the conversation. I put my hands on the round rise of my stomach and whispered to my unborn son that I would do the right thing for him. I would not be forced to decide. Rob had been inside my head, convincing me. After that night, I prepared to decide on my own. I knew that if I was to live with myself, I would have to be certain that I made the best and right choice for my son and not anyone else, including me. It was a lot to bear, but it was good. It gave me strength.

Up until that night, I felt I needed Rob. I needed his protection, support and help. But somewhere in the middle of our closet conversation, I suddenly did not care what he thought or wanted. I wasn't scared of what he might do to me, because he wasn't with me. He was back in Newfoundland, at home, saving face. If I decided to keep my baby, then he could be damned. Not. His. Fucking. Business.

After, I made more of an effort to examine my feelings as I worked towards a decision. Sr. R had been urging me to uncover any doubts or misgivings, and they poured out of me in my counselling sessions. My pre-rehearsed speeches about "definitely" placing my baby for adoption were replaced with my acknowledgement that I was sad, uncertain and afraid. I needed to figure out what I wanted to do. I did not know if giving up my son was possible. I embraced uncertainty. I shut out the carefully concocted logic and reason to let my emotions come into focus. I asked questions with my heart instead of my head. I forced myself to face the disturbing, harrowing fact that I was about to give up a little human being. Sr. R patiently listened as my words and tears broke the seal of my facade and honesty emerged.

It was a long way back from indecision to certainty. I weighed the odds, thinking about what his life would be with me, a single mother, versus having two parents. I did not want to him to be hurt by the rejection and denial that seemed inevitable from his father's family. I wanted to give him the best life possible, the happiest. That meant taking me out of the scenario. Did I feel good about that? Not for one second. It hurt like hell and does to this very minute.

I insisted on being a part of choosing my son's parents, something that had not been previously permitted. I demanded it. I needed to know what kind of people would be raising my son. While I did not know who they were, I knew enough about them to be sure of the life they could provide to a child.

Initially, I wanted to meet, interview and vet them. Sr. R said that they would not stand up to my expectations, no matter who they were. It was a sage point that I have thought about many times. Back then, keeping the parents and the birth mother separate was seen as setting the stage for a clean break and successful adoption. Still, I wonder. What story might I tell now if I had met them? Would I have looked at those two hopeful parents and said, "No, not good enough—I can do as well?"

My father once told me, "In life, for the most part, be nice. But when you want something, and you know you are right, fight to make it happen. Stand up for what you believe in, even if you stand alone." True to his lesson, I became a woman that pushes hard when I want something. It is a tactic that sometimes shocks people and gets their undivided attention. People take me to be quiet and soft-spoken. When I show up like Beowulf, wielding my tongue as a sword, they are surprised, but often impressed too. Sr. R saw that in me and went along with my request. It was 1983, for God's sake! Sr. R worried that no matter what I knew about the adopting parents there would always be reasons to find fault and disapprove. I insisted that I "would know." And I did know, as did Sr. R, when the right parents showed up.

we are
the broken many
walking in daylight
and darkness
with a secret
that destroys us
we don't
need your pity
or want it
we ask
only to be heard
we need to feel
and be real
repair as best we can
in search of wholeness
and personal forgiveness
we walk
among you
and know
that you too
have a story
to tell

babysitters' club

There was a tradition at the Home of the Guardian Angel I found odd: the residents were invited to babysit children in the neighbourhood. I found it ironic that girls hiding out in a home for unwed mothers, intending to give up our babies, would be considered suitable to take care of other mothers' children. Or was there an ulterior motive? Perhaps taking care of children could give us the opportunity to evaluate if we in fact wanted to keep our babies or solidify the certainty that we desired no part of being mothers. In either case, better to be sure than still waffling at the point of delivery.

I thought it a cruel imposition that did not consider the distress that could result. We had come to Halifax to escape scrutiny; now we were expected to enter the homes of married, committed parents and take care of their young ones.

The mothers, presumably part of some program run by the church, visited one morning, bringing their babies and toddlers with them. Suddenly the usually quiet sitting room was filled with diaper bags, colourful toys and kids sitting, crawling and tumbling over the laps and legs of the moms. The mothers chattered eagerly. The kids babbled, cried and smiled. We sat on the outskirts of the group, looking on with interest and trepidation. This was the test run to find out who was who and how things would work. It seemed to me that the mothers were relieved that they had their kids to focus on, so they didn't have to look too closely at us. We sat in our plump embarrassment, watching these happy young moms with their kids. They tried desperately to act positive and accepting. We wanted desperately to escape.

Sr. M stood in the middle, assuring the moms that we were willing to look after their little darlings. She was uncomfortable, her laughter forced and slightly nervous. She looked keen to get this meeting to its conclusion.

I took in the scene and wondered yet again how I ended up there. Just a few months before, I had been discussing literature. I hated the looks of pity those moms had for us. The sideways glances at our stomachs. I felt like one of them might lay a hand upon my arm, pat me and tell me I was making the right decision to give up my baby since I was ill prepared to raise him myself. I wondered if some of the babes on the floor were adopted, maybe from the Home of the Guardian Angel. Were these the good mothers, the better choices, who got to raise them?

I wanted to tell them that I was educated, smart. Better than what they thought of me. I did not have the personal fortitude to walk away. I sat there and participated and felt like shit. I looked at their babies and felt small and sad. The glowing happiness of motherhood made me want to cry. I despised their pity and their happiness because it flung my predicament in my face. I was not a project or a church mission. I was a young woman with a heart and a story they knew nothing about and would never know.

Soon after our little get-together, Sr. M came to ask me to babysit for one of those moms. I politely agreed, without revealing my apprehension. Sr. M said that I was one of the most responsible of the girls and she knew I would do well. She did not ask me how I felt about it—she just reminded me not to be late and said I might want to leave a little early.

She walked away, leaving me looking at the piece of paper on which the address and other details were written. I had never liked babysitting. When I was a teenager, babysitting was at the bottom of my list of ways to make spending money. It was way too much work for too little cash. The door closed behind the parents and the kids lifted off into a whirlwind of destructive antics. They sucked down junk food when I wasn't looking, body-surfed on the stairs, made bouncy castles out of the couch and screamed when I tried to round them up for bed. When they finally crashed from exhaustion, I settled in for the long wait until the parents returned, which was often in the early hours of the morning. As soon as they finally came through the door, I would race home to my bed, cursing the fact that they had underpaid me or promised to send the money to my house the next day. What kind of people hired a babysitter without having cash on hand? Parents of maniac kids, that's who. I would vow every time never to babysit again.

The next day, I arrived early so that I could meet the kids and be given instructions for my duties. Right away I could see that their home was well lived in, wholesome in a way that spoke of organic, healthy food. It smelled of homemade bread and freshly made coffee. The mom met me at the door and rushed me into the kitchen where she was feeding her kids lunch.

I sat at the wooden kitchen table with them, in a sunny room where toys littered the floor from a recent playtime. A window seat at the back of the kitchen was a cozy nook of blankets, pillows and books. The mom was tall, blond and pretty and the kids, two sweet little girls, had chubby cheeks and rosy complexions. They were happy, curious and reached out to offer me food from their sticky hands. I could not help but smile at the little charmers. I exhaled my nervousness, trying to relax as the mom explained what the girls liked and where everything was that I might need while she was gone. Then she gathered her things, kissed the girls on their heads and waved bye-bye to them as she scurried out the door.

Alone now with two small girls, I wondered if I could handle things. The mom had pinned instructions on the fridge, and there were a couple of numbers to call in case of emergency. God, I hoped there would not be an emergency.

The girls were about two and three years old, close in age and size. Their mom gone, they were no longer interested in eating, so I washed their faces and hands, pulled them from their chairs and relocated them to the floor near the window seat. I gathered toys and books and set about to entertain them. They liked me right away. They plopped down in my lap, tugged at my glasses and stuck their fingers in my curls. They got up close to my face and whispered in my ear as though telling secrets. They were adorable, easy and well-mannered for such little people.

I built a tent under the kitchen chairs with a blanket and pillows, making a little nest for the three of us. The girls lay close to me, and I could smell baby shampoo and applesauce. Their tiny hands were soft and warm. Their eyes widened as I read and created voices for the characters in the stories. They giggled and asked for another story every time we finished one.

Time went by unnoticed, and before I knew it, their mom was home. The kids ran to greet her, and she kissed them on their heads, asking them if they had been good girls. They chorused "yes!" and I confirmed that they were. Their mom thanked me profusely and marvelled at our tent and the girls' contentment. She pressed twenty dollars into my hands and overruled my objections, insisting that it was worth much more. She hoped I would come again. I did not want the money, which made me feel like I was thirteen, but I also did not want to offend her. I pushed it deep in my pocket. We walked to the front door, the little girls holding my hands and tugging me along as I giggled at their playfulness.

I had begrudgingly come to the house like a sentenced criminal, resentful because I felt I had little to no choice. Yet, I reluctantly left the warmth of the kitchen and the snuggles of those small girls. It was the closest I had come to family in some time. I enjoyed being in a house where contentment was evident in the details of the messy kitchen and the sweetness of two little people. I walked slowly back to the Home, perplexed by the unexpected gift of comfort.

When I remember that babysitting adventure, I think I had it in me, always, to be a good mother. As young as I was, I already knew what children needed. I have never spoken of that day to anyone. It accentuated my regret because I could have been that kind of mother for my son. He was with me that day, carried tenderly inside me. My ease in taking care of those little girls made me uneasy. I both liked and hated myself for it. I did not have the husband or the house, but I had the mother in me to create a home and a way forward.

It was my only babysitting assignment, and I never saw that mom or her girls again. The details are vague now, but I think I delivered and left soon after. I saw it as one of those events in my life that came about to teach me something important—that although I was not ready to be a mother, I was not unable.

The babysitting tradition at the Home was something I hated. And needed. And live with.

I gave up my son because I wanted him to have that mom, that kitchen, that home. I wanted him welcomed into the world by two parents. I did not want him to lack or struggle. I signed his life over with hope and belief that he would be happy.

I could not offer him security. It was 1983. Single mothers were still not treated kindly or given easy access to opportunities. An uphill climb with me was not something I wanted for him. And truthfully, not something I wanted for myself, because the way seemed impossible.

Yet, I wanted to make tents out of blankets and tell stories inside them. Stories that I created out of the air and whispered in his ear right before sleeping. I wanted to feel his sticky fingers wrapped around my own. I wanted his smiles and giggles. I wanted him to call me Momma. I wanted him for my own.

But the past cannot be rewritten. In the years since, that day in a tent with two little girls represents what I gave up and lost. It was a snapshot of the yielded possible.

tell me your terrifying
let me see you
not as you choose
to appear
but as you really are
with your scars
apparent
and your wishes
rising
from outstretched palms
let me listen
to your honesty
here in the dusty desert
of your truth
where your dreams
can still flourish
like cactus flowers
against the odds
and because
there is beauty in you
waiting
to burst free
tell me your terrifying
let me see you
as you
are meant to be seen

bee my friend

I first saw her with her parents and Sr. M in the special room reserved for visitors. As I passed down the hall and looked in, Bee caught my eye. She had the expression of someone who had found herself in the most distressing conversation and wished only for it to end. I could see that Bee was younger than me, but her poise suggested a maturity beyond her years. She was pretty, with soft brown hair and a clear, fresh complexion. Her belly was round inside a delicate summer blouse with printed flowers. Instantly I thought, "I like her."

I needed a friend. I needed someone I could genuinely identify with and have thoughtful conversations. Until Bee came, I had been lonely and mostly isolated. I sat with the other girls to watch television, passing the time between meals or outings to prenatal classes at the hospital. But there had not been interest in anything deeper than basic talk about food preparation or setting and clearing the table. We were together but separate. I knew very little about these girls, as was the unspoken agreement among us. It was as though we never got past the introductions, names and where we were from. Their stories came and left with them, untold and unheard.

When Bee walked in, her eyes told me that she was searching for someone she could befriend and trust. It did not take long for us to connect and start talking. She told me she was in high school and getting pregnant was not part of the plan. Her boyfriend was still in the picture, but she had, as usual, borne the brunt of the blame. His parents were protective of him and accused her of screwing up; they did not want her ruining their son's future. It was hard on her, but she had the support of her parents. She had come to the Home to escape the harshness of the community, and so that she could have the counselling and care they provided.

Bee and I took a lot of long walks that fall. The neighbourhoods of Halifax were beautiful with the browns, golds, oranges and reds of autumn. Many afternoons, once lunch was over and everything cleared away, she and I would head out. We walked with the sun warming us while we kicked our feet through fallen leaves. We talked about anything and everything. Together we could just be girls, sharing hopes, dreams and ideas. It was a friendship born out of circumstances but bonded by mutual interests and genuine liking of one another. Bee was extraordinary, I knew. I felt that, in the future, she would be brave and bold. She would take control of her destiny because shining from her was the strength of character that revealed a clever, resourceful person.

On our walks, we laughed about funny things happening at the Home. Being able to walk away for a couple of hours made it all more bearable. Sr. M was intense on the best of days, and we giggled endlessly about her quirkiness. We would feel badly, momentarily, for gossiping about her—then we would look at each other and laughingly agree that it was impossible not to.

Bee took the room on the same floor as me, the one with two beds and lots of light coming in from two large windows. I spent time in there with her, talking well into the evenings. It was fun to have a friend that I could talk to and be silly with. Our days were otherwise endlessly the same, so I waited anxiously for our walks and to hang out in her room. We never ran out of things to say or laugh about.

I went to Bee's room the night I went into labour. I had been feeling off during dinner, unable to eat much. At first, the pains were barely noticeable, but by early evening they were becoming intense and somewhat regular. I knocked on Bee's door to say, "I think I am in labour." She grabbed my arm and pulled me quickly inside. Bee enjoyed nothing more than a project. She sat perched on her bed observing me closely, pen poised and ready to write in her notebook. Whenever a contraction started, I paced back and forth between the two beds, unable to sit or stay still.

This went on for some time, with Bee exclaiming time and length between contractions as they grew closer and closer together. She was jubilant over the record she was building and from time to time she bounced up off the bed, excited to be a part of the unfolding drama that was my labour. What we did not account for was that Sr. M's room was directly beneath us. While we were tabulating results, she was below us listening to the incessant creaking and banging on the floor above her head.

Suddenly, the door flew open, and there she stood in her dressing gown and slippers. She glared at the two of us and barked, "What is going on in here!?! One of you had better be in labour!" I stood in the middle of the room clutching my stomach, the edge of the last contraction just wearing off and fearing the next. After a moment of shock, Bee regained her composure and sprang from her bed, shoving her notebook in front of Sr. M. and declaring, "Mary is in labour! And look, I have been recording her contractions. They are getting a lot closer together. See!"

That news hit Sr. M like a bolt. She turned to me and demanded, "Why did you not come to my room to get me? I told you that if you go into labour you are to come and knock on my door." I was still speechless, so she continued, "Get dressed. Get your suitcase and meet me downstairs. We have to get you to the hospital straight away." She turned and left, leaving the door open. As she went down the stairs, she called up, "And hurry!" Bee and I looked at each other. We could not help but laugh. Then another contraction hit, and I ran to my room, clutching myself and suddenly fearing what now was in motion.

Back in my room, between contractions, I managed to get out of my nightgown and into regular clothes. I pulled my small suitcase from under the bed. Thankfully, I had had the foresight to pack in preparation for the hospital. Sr. M tapped on my door. I was worried that she was still cross and wondered what she would hurl at me next. Instead, when I opened the door, I could see that her manner had softened. She smiled kindly and asked if I was ready. I said I was, and she took my suitcase. The same suitcase she had carried up the stairs on my arrival, which seemed far in the past. She looked at me then and said, "Everything will be all right. Are you okay?" I nodded yes despite feeling anything but okay.

As we walked down the hall to the stairs, Bee emerged from her room. I could see worry in her eyes. She smiled and reached out to hug me. I quickly embraced my friend. I was grateful that she had been there throughout the evening and to keep me laughing through the steady onset of contractions. Perhaps all women remember the details of their first labour. I have so many reasons to remember mine. Among them is Bee, who was funny and encouraging. I was glad I had not gone directly to Sr. M. That would have created a far more serious unfolding of events, with a lot more fear.

I don't recall if I saw any of the other girls on the way out. Sr. M and I paused as a contraction hit, but finally, we were out the door and in her car. It occurred to me that I did not really know her much better than when I had first arrived. She remained aloof and distant. I had never confided in her and yet I was about to deliver a baby in her presence. I had to trust her to get me through the most momentous experience of my life. As we drove, she told me about what would happen when we walked in. I half listened. I was consumed by pain, fear and vulnerability. My jovial hours with Bee were replaced with the impending reality that a baby would soon be born. My pregnancy was about to end.

*her strength lay
along the length
of her spine
that over time
held her in poise
especially
on the days
she felt spineless
and guileless
but stood
in the could
and did it
anyway*

deliver me

I sat on the edge of a small, plastic chair with one hand on my belly and the other gripping the desk in front of me. The hospital receiving clerk had a long form and was asking me a string of questions that she said I had to answer before she could send me to a room. I winced and tried my best to focus on what she was asking. Sr. M stood beside me, and I sensed her irritation, which I hoped was not directed towards me. After a time, she let out a heavy sigh and leaned across the desk, her two stout arms pushing her forward, as she let loose on the clerk. "Can't you see this young girl is in labour!?! We are not going to answer any more questions until she is made comfortable. Get her into a bed and send someone to complete the forms after that!" The clerk drew away from Sr. M in apparent alarm and began to protest, saying this was the required procedure. Sr. M insisted, "Now!" The clerk jumped up from her station and returned with a nurse who led us to my room. Sr. M had a fire in her. I was surprised and grateful to get off that chair and out of the hallway.

I thought, based on the frequency, timing and intensity of my con-tractions, that delivery would start almost immediately when we got to the hospital. I was shaking as I undressed and got into the green hospital gown. Panic had a grip on me and would not let go. However, I was told to get into bed so that my attending nurse could see how far my cervix was dilated. I knew from prenatal classes that the magic number was ten centimetres. That was when the cervix was fully open (God help me!!), and I would be ready to push and deliver the baby. The pushing part was the crux of my fear. I knew I had to push a baby, a human being, out through my vagina. It seemed impossible that a baby, no matter how small, could come through that tender, sheltered opening in my body. In prenatal class, our instructor had been very deliberate in emphasizing the wonder of the body to open and provide space for the baby to come out. "The bones of the pelvis shift and move!" she explained with a tone of forced excitement. I am a small person. How much moving was required, I wondered? And would I fail? Would the doctor have to slice into my uterus and yank the baby out because my pelvic bones refused to shift? I thought of my mom and hoped again that I was like her in this way.

When the nurse came in, she pulled back the sheet and placed each of my heels in stirrups. (I hated those stirrups. Still do. There is nothing about that position that is comfortable or comforting to a woman.) She asked me to shimmy my bottom down to the edge of the bed. With latex gloves on, she pushed her fingers inside me. I stared at the ceiling, agonized that this nurse was exploring my vagina. She poked around in there and then drew back as she pulled off her gloves and declared, "Six centimetres. And your water has not broken. Lots of time yet."

I did not know if this was good or unwelcome news. Considering the pain and regular arrival of contractions, I wanted a deadline. Something like "twenty minutes to full dilation." One hour to delivery. I asked, "How long?" She replied, "Don't know. Hard to say. You are all different. We will let the contractions run their course and, if need be, we will break your water to move things along." Then she looked at Sr. M, who was standing beside my bed, to tell her she could go home. They would call her when it was getting close to time. The way she said it made apparent the number of times she had seen Sr. M in this scenario. Another pregnant, unwed mother about to give birth.

Sr. M reassured me that she would be back well in time for the delivery. I did not want to be alone, but I was not sure it appropriate to ask her to stay or if I even really wanted her there. I knew that she had had no sleep and it was well past her usual bedtime. She left. The nurse said that, because of the level of pain I was having with my contractions, she would order an epidural so that I would be able to rest and get some sleep. While that sounded like a promising idea, it made me wonder just how long this would take. I had made it through nine months only to find that the last hours of my pregnancy would be the longest, most unbearable stretch of time.

Suddenly, I was alone in a small hospital room. The plain, white walls, white sheets and white tables blurred into a seamless, shapeless background. The child inside me was making his way into the world. I thought of my parents at home in their house, sleeping in their bed, oblivious to what was happening to their daughter. I had the urge to call them and blurt out my situation. Once again, I longed for my mother. I wanted her to stroke my head, sit close to me and tell me it would be okay. I did not consider, until many years later, the gravity of the risk I took. If anything had gone wrong, it would have been a complete shock to my family. I have been told that I was courageous. But I was not. I was scared and alone. I was frightened that night as I had not been before and have not been since.

I was shaking uncontrollably. My teeth chattered and my legs vibrated. No matter how I tried to calm myself, the shaking seemed to get worse. The door opened, and another nurse came in. She was small and sweet and cute. She came to tell me that the epidural had been ordered and that she would stay with me until then. She noticed how badly I was shaking and left to get blankets. She returned with a bundle of warm flannel covers, spreading them over me and tucking them tightly under me. The warmth of those blankets felt so good they made me cry. They reminded me of my mother and how she had made up my bed with cozy flannel sheets at Christmas, less than a year ago.

The nurse leaned over me with a look of concern and asked if I was okay. I blinked away my tears and, in a trembling voice, told her that I was scared. I asked her why I could not stop shaking. I wanted to know if it was normal. She pulled a chair up beside my bed and put her hand on my blanketed arm. "It happens," she said. "Your body is moving into labour now. It has a lot going on." The heated blankets slowed the tremors, and I was able to quiet myself between contractions. Seeing my distress, the nurse said that she would stay with me until I went to the delivery room. I was so grateful I started crying again.

Inserting the epidural took some time and effort. I had to lie on my side with my back exposed so that the needle could be placed at the exact right spot in my spine. With the blankets pulled back, I started to shake violently once more. I needed to be perfectly still so the anesthesiologist could insert the injection without damage to my spine. I think today I would say forget it. I would not take that kind of risk but would endure the pain instead. The young me just wanted the pain to stop. The nurse spoke to me gently, coaching me to relax, focus and reach a place of calm. We needed the perfect moment when I was not shaking or having a contraction. Miraculously, the opportunity finally arrived, and the needle slid into the exact location. What happened behind me I did not see, nor did I want to see, but the anesthesiologist finally announced, "Success!" He told me I did a great job and soon after the sharp edge of the contractions subsided.

He left, and the nurse brought more warm blankets for me. I lay back on the pillows, once again feeling like a stranger in my own life. I was in a hospital bed at the Grace Maternity Hospital in Halifax. I was having a baby with a kind nurse beside me and not another soul to comfort me. All through that night, my legs shook, and the shaking rippled throughout my body. The epidural eased the pain of the contractions so that in between them I drifted off to sleep.

It was long past midnight, and I was exhausted. It seemed a long time since I had gone to Bee's room. As each contraction started, I would wake and tell the nurse, "I am having another one." I think she kept track of them. As the night wore on, with me sleeping and waking, she took care of me. She talked to me, her voice a gentle whisper in the silent room. Several times I asked her to please not leave me alone, and she assured me she wouldn't. When the first grey light of day pushed in around the window shades, I was fully awake, aware that the epidural was wearing off. I knew that when the pain returned, the shaking would resume.

"When do you think I will go to the delivery room?" I nervously asked her. She responded, "I think soon. I need to see how far you are dilated now." I was at ten centimetres, but my water had still not broken. She called in another nurse who used an instrument that looked like a crochet hook, and a great, hot rush of liquid fell between my legs and feet. It was an odd sensation of relief followed by an immediate increase in contractions. The night nurse told me then that it was time for her to go off shift. She explained that I would be moved soon to the OR. "It is time," she said, smiling at me. "It is time." Those words were the defining line between being pregnant with my son and no longer being pregnant with my son. The nine months that I carried him, he was mine. He was with me. I was his mother. I took care of him and loved the movement and feel of him inside me. With the words "it is time," my time with him was coming to an end.

I don't know the medical reason that I trembled all through that night. I am sure it could be explained. In my interpretation, I shook with sadness. It was the beginning of loss. The birth of a child should herald the beginning of motherhood. It was not that for me. And I knew in those final hours that when the time came, and he was delivered into the world, I would lose him. The decision had been made. I'd committed to following through on the plan. Another woman and her husband would be his parents. I shook out of fear for what I had to face, out of sadness and out of wishing to God that I could lock into the present moment and not have to go forward.

"It is time." The beginning of the end for me.

If I knew the name of the nurse who stayed with me that night I have long since forgotten it. There have been times that I wondered if she was real or if I dreamed her; if she was an angel. Perhaps she was my grandmother, who loved me in the same gentle way and let me wear her silky bed jacket in her featherbed on the Saturday nights I slept at her house. She would tuck me in during the second intermission of the *Hockey Night in Canada* game, kissing me on my forehead before she went back to the couch with her knitting. I fell asleep to my grandmother shouting at the Toronto Maple Leafs and Montreal Canadiens—she knew all the names of the players. I swear she could knit an entire sock during a heated hockey period. The more excited she got, the faster the rows appeared.

Yes, my grandmother was the angel I would have chosen that night. How often as a child I had run to her with bumps or bruises or hurt feelings, seeking her solace.

Thinking that the nurse somehow embodied my grandmother was the kind of magic I believed in as a girl. I thought my grandmother could do anything and make everyone better. She was a constant source of certain love and approval. The last time I saw her, she was in her wooden rocking chair, where she'd rocked me and let me cry on her shoulder and told me stories of her life, my eyes wide in wonder. In her will, she left me the rocking chair because it was the one thing that I wanted from her house. It is in my kitchen now, and when I look at it, I see the small, sprightly woman whose love for me was shelter and safety.

Suddenly, Sr. M was back in the room, and a new bed was wheeled in to take me to the delivery room. My labour pains were now one on top of the other, and I had my first instinct to push, which I yelled out. The new attending nurse ordered me not to push, not yet. If I could have reached her, I would have swatted her. I felt like hitting someone, anyone who told me not to push, so great was the urge.

It was a bright, sunny October morning outside, a Saturday. The door opened, and then I was in the hallway watching the ceiling lights and tiles go by, one after the other, as they wheeled me to the OR. Sr. M walked beside me, silently holding onto the bedrail. I was crossing the line from one time into the next. I was a patient on a gurney. I was at the mercy of doctors and nurses and destiny. I was about to see my son.

The OR was green. Green walls, green sheets, green scrubs on the doctors and nurses. The room was filled with people, all waiting for me. My bed was pushed into the center of the room and the wheels locked to hold it firmly in place. I was draped in green sheets and my feet raised into those awful stirrups. Between the tremors and the contractions, I had little concern about what was being done to me. Sr. M leaned over to give me a look of reassurance. The doctor, who I had not seen before, was orchestrating. He stood at the end of the bed and spoke to me overtop the green sheets. He said it was time to start pushing as soon as the next contraction began. It came. I pushed. I leaned hard into it. The brief pause that followed each push gave me just enough time to breathe before the next one came. Somehow, thankfully, I did not need those breathing lessons from prenatal class. I was pushing and bearing the pain.

After a few more pushes, the head was out and with a final, gentle push, the whole body emerged. There was a flurry of activity at the end of the bed. The doctor announced that it was a boy and held the baby up to place him on my skin. I held up my hands instinctively to take him. He was crying and moving and small and red with lots of dark hair and ...

Sr. M's hand shot between us, shaking her head, motioning for the doctor to take the baby away. She quietly explained, "She is giving the baby up for adoption." The doctor's smile disappeared, and he turned away with my son and gave him to a nurse who took him out of the room.

My son was out of my body. Out of my reach.

I remember
the moment you were born
the doctor said, it's a boy
your first gasping cry
your small plump body
the cord connecting us
clamped and cut
the shrunken hollow of my stomach
where you had been
the fierce shrieking need
to see you
and hold you
pushing down that need
swallowing that need
along with my tears
and my brokenness
as they carried you away
hearing someone say, she's not keeping him
and then the silence
as I lay there numb
suddenly alone
so much pain
to bring you into the world
nothing compared
to the pain of letting you go

I remember
the moment you were born
I remember

after birth

Sr. M stood beside me, not saying a word. The doctor explained that I needed to push a few more times to deliver the afterbirth. I complied. Then he stitched the episiotomy. I could feel a pool of sticky blood around my bottom, but I didn't care. It took a long time for the doctor to complete the stitching. I lay under the ugly green sheet with my hands pressed onto the slack cavity where my son had been. I was empty. I could not speak. I could not cry. I lay bearing the unbearable. It is the part of my story that is the hardest to write and the most difficult to remember. I hate myself and yet I want to go back to that self and put my arms around me in the loving embrace that no one offered that day. As I looked around the OR, it was a scene of cleaning up and putting things back in order. All signs of the miracle of birth and the joy of that were absent. I had become the birth mother, the one who gave up her child.

When my son was taken from the room, I lost not only him but also myself.

Eventually, I was taken to a semi-private ward on another floor in the hospital. I was the only patient in the room, which was a relief. I did not want anyone asking questions. The sun shone brightly, warming the bed sheets and pillow. I asked the nurse to pull the shades. The sky's cheerfulness seemed to mock my sadness. I settled into the bed and instantly fell asleep. I slept for hours. In the afternoon, Bee and some of the other girls came to visit. They were happy to see me but seemed hesitant to ask questions about how everything had gone. They too had to face labour and delivery. We talked about mundane things until it was time for them to head back. I was grateful for the company and surprised that a few of the girls had made the effort to accompany Bee.

As the day went on, I thought of home and Rob. I shoved my feet into my slippers several times and shuffled down the hall to call him. No answer. My heart sunk. I stood in the hospital phonebooth, wearing a sad pink robe and slippers borrowed from the Home's shared clothing closet. "The least he could fucking do for me is pick up the fucking phone," I thought.

After multiple frustrating tries, he picked up. I wanted to scream—where the hell had he been all day while I was in labour and delivering our son? He had no way to know, of course, but then he knew very little about what was occurring with me day to day in Halifax. I knew he would not show up in person, but I wanted and believed I deserved a place in his thoughts.

"Where were you?" I asked.

"Playing tennis, and then we ..."

"I had the baby today."

Silence.

"Do you want to know what it is?"

"No, I ..."

"It's a boy. I had a baby boy. We have a baby boy."

Silence.

I waited.

"Are you okay?" he asked finally.

"No."

Silence.

"I just called to let you know that it's over."

That was essentially our conversation. I hung up the phone, opened the door of the phone booth and shuffled back to my room in my fuzzy pink slippers. I lay on the bed with night pressing in around me. I was relieved to have told him. Off in the distance, I could vaguely hear nurses talking at the desk and the occasional ding of the elevator arriving on our floor.

I sat up. The elevator. I swung my legs over the side of the bed and pushed my feet back into the slippers. I hurried down the hall and headed directly to the elevator.

After a couple of errors, I found the floor with the nursery. The lights were turned down low. I came up to the window and stood looking in at the sleeping babies. There were a lot of them. I walked to the door and went in. To my left, a nurse looked up from her work at a desk. "Are you here to see your baby?" she asked. I indicated yes. "Name?" I was puzzled. "What's your last name?" "Hodder," I responded. The nurse left her station and came towards me. She did not ask me any further questions as it seemed she understood my situation. She told me to follow her and took me to the far back corner of the nursery. She stopped beside his little bed, a small see-through plastic bed with a tiny bundle wrapped in a white and yellow blanket inside. The nurse leaned over him and smiled, turning to say that he was a good baby, hardly a peep out of him. I stood waiting, looking, barely able to breathe. She gave my arm a little squeeze and said, "I will leave you. Take your time."

Then I was alone with my son. He slept peacefully. His cheeks were round and rosy, framed by a mass of dark hair. I stood looking at him, taking him in. Slowly, I reached out and tugged away the blanket so that I could see all of him. I looked at his fingers and his toes and the length of him. I leaned close to smell his baby scent. He squirmed and stretched in his sleep, making little noises. I touched the softness of him. I stroked his small hands and as I did his fingers reflexively gripped my index finger. If a touch can stop a heart, surely this was it.

I whispered, "I am your mother."

I told him I loved him. I explained that what I was doing, giving him up, was for him. His happiness, his well-being, his life. I told him that it was not going to be easy, but I would face the future without him. Somehow. I asked him not to forget me. I tried to imprint on him the love I was feeling, in hopes that it would remain with him in the years ahead. I kissed his tiny brow, and for a long, long time I just breathed into the silence so that I would not lose my mind. The temptation to hold him overwhelmed me. But I knew that if I gave into that temptation, I would never let him go. Slowly, meticulously, lovingly, I replaced the blanket, carefully tucking it around him so as not to wake him. He was perfect. He was mine.

Those were our only moments together. A few brief moments to see him, touch him and be his mother. I am grateful that I thought to find him that night. It was something I had to do. I had to see him and talk to him. There was no one to advise or dissuade me. I had a window of time and I took it.

I wonder if he felt my presence and if that feeling remained with him as I intended. Great and wonderful things can happen in a few moments. They did for me in those moments—he was real and present, small and perfect. I placed my hands on him and felt his breath and warmth. In his face, I saw my own. If you ask me how I could walk away from him, I cannot answer. I don't know how. I only know that I did.

I returned to my hospital room. I climbed back into bed. I pulled the covers over me and looked out at the night with the moon and the stars in the sky. It was October 8, 1983. I would like to say there was peace in the stillness. But that would not be true. There was calm, a feeling of having come through a storm and survived. I had delivered my son into the world. He was healthy and whole. I was okay, physically. No caesarean and only a few stitches. From that day on he and I would exist in the world together even though we would do it separately. From that day on I have called him my son, even as he calls another woman his mother.

I was awake for a long time, lost in my private celebration of having given my son life. Despite my intentions, I was proud that the small perfect baby a few floors up was my doing. I marvelled at what my body had done, holding, nourishing and cradling him into a living being. For the previous five years, while I had studied for my degree, I thought the most important learning happened in classrooms. Yet here I was, at the end of a day in which I had given birth. I marvelled at the boy who had come through me. From the outset, his life brought lessons unparalleled by anything else that had happened in my first twenty-two years.

you cannot
see me
I hide
in here
inside me
where it's safe

I look
ok to you
a disguise
for your eyes
that I
created diligently

if you
could see me
you might be sad
I cannot allow that
this pain
is mine

I sometimes
fool myself
as I walk about
looking out
from caged
windows

and you
admire my form
pretty face
not a trace
of what
destroys me

careful what you wish for

My body went back to its pre-baby shape with no effort at all. The blessing of being young and fit, I suppose. Within days, my stomach was almost as taut as it was before I got pregnant. Sr. R exclaimed that you could not even tell that I had had a baby. It was what I had hoped for, yet I was disappointed. A part of me wanted proof of what I had endured and accomplished. It was the dichotomy of my predicament: I had hidden a pregnancy but wanted recognition for it. It annoyed me that people would look at me and see me as just another young woman with a slim figure. I was now so much more than that.

A baby had emerged from my womb! A boy with chubby cheeks, big dark eyes and soft brown hair. His skin felt like silk and smelled indescribably sweet. I had listened to him breathing, a gentle whisper that rose and fell from his tiny chest. It made me fall in love with him like no one ever before. He was small, beautiful and a reflection of me. He was a part of me, flesh of my flesh, heart of my heart.

The day after delivery, a nurse came to tell me that it was time to bind my breasts and begin sitz baths, procedures that no one had mentioned in prenatal class. The look on my face told her I was confused.

She explained that a sitz bath was a warm, saltwater bath to help heal the swelling and stitches left by the episiotomy and lessen scarring. Since I would not be breastfeeding, my breasts had to be bound to halt the milk flow and avoid engorgement, which would be extremely uncomfortable. I needed to avoid that.

She bound my breasts with a long strip of cotton fabric that she wound around me several times. I was embarrassed to be naked in front of her, but she went about her task indifferently while the bath ran. I tried not to look at her. It hurt and when I winced, she said, without apology, "It needs to be tight. If it's not tight enough it won't work." She tugged the fabric and tucked the end up under the binding at the back. I stood in awkward silence wondering how I was to take a bath without getting the cotton wet. Not sensing sympathy, I kept that concern to myself.

When the bath was ready, she stepped out. I locked the door behind her and lowered myself into the water. Feeling pathetic and alone, I cried. My breasts hurt. I wanted to tear off the binding. I wanted to scream into the echoing starkness of that small bathroom until the walls shook. I would not breastfeed my son. The weight of that hit me. He was in the nursery. What were they feeding him? I remembered my mother saying that breast milk is the best milk for babies. And here I was sitting in a bathtub forcibly restraining the natural flow of milk that was meant to feed him. I had not considered that the milk would come once I had given birth. My body was doing what it was meant to do, which was to create nourishment for my child. I was interrupting the natural course of events, keeping milk from the baby who needed it.

I sat in the bath carefully pushing the water in and out, over and over my legs, in a pattern of waves.

Within a couple of days, the binding worked. My milk was gone. My episiotomy healed quickly. With several sitz baths each day, water, salt and tears washed it away. My body was restored to its slender, small-chested, perfect vagina state, the mystery of childbirth safely hidden inside me. I was like a house cleaned and scrubbed and set in order, pleasing to observe unless you opened a closet and the stuff pushed inside suddenly fell out in a mess.

The times I spent alone in that bath were some of the saddest I have ever experienced. They were the end of my pregnancy. I faced the part of myself that could go through with a life-altering plan to give up a child. I became the girl who could squeeze shut the milk flow in her breasts, the keeper of secrets, one who fooled others but not herself. I knew that I could steal away to Halifax and have a child and give that child up, but that everything that happened to me would remain in me no matter how well I hid it. I was a sad girl sitting alone in the bath, naked and afraid. Clean on the outside but feeling forever soiled on the inside.

A few of the girls came to visit me again, and some eventually asked how it went and if I was relieved it was over. Curiosity got the better of them. One girl remarked that she wished she was done and that she envied me. I put on a brave face and encouraged her, saying that the time would go by quickly. I could not speak of how I really felt, nor that relief had not come. They would have to face their truth soon enough.

As they gathered around my hospital bed, it felt like a slumber party with an unfortunate theme. Unwed mothers talking about delivering a baby that was nowhere in sight. No cards, flowers, little baby onesies, blue "it's-a-boy" balloons, no pictures. Gloom and hope hung in the air, tied not to string but to my heart. A club for the outcast. The girls complimented me on how great I looked. It did not help, because for the first time ever, how I felt mattered much more than how I looked. My body was not the same. Nothing about me was the same. I was broken and that anyone could look at me and not recognize that seemed impossible.

My public freedom was reinstated. I could go anywhere without having to drape myself in awful, shapeless clothes. I could recover my skinny jeans from the bottom of the closet when I got home, slip into them and zip them up without a struggle. I could go anywhere and mingle in the crowds. That was what I had been waiting for. That was what I had asked Jesus for that all those nights in the bathroom. I would have sold my soul to the devil for it. I had endured seclusion, dreaming about the day I could resume my normal life.

Unexpectedly, hiding my pregnancy seemed insignificant compared to what I now concealed. This was a much more agonizing secret. Before it was the shame of being pregnant and the fear of being caught. Now there was a child. My son. In the world. I had brought him here. It was never about the pregnancy. It was about a child. A boy with my hair that looked like me. You can hide a pregnancy. I did that. But you cannot hide a child. A child that I loved and adored long before he was born and ever so much more deeply from the moment I saw him.

Yet, I was about to give him to another that he would come to call mother. He would bond with her. She would rock him to sleep, change his diapers. She would soothe his tears and bathe him and kiss him and see all his firsts: first tooth, first word, first step. And I would be alone, looking like a typical young girl, but being nothing of the sort. What could not be seen was the real me, the best and worst of me. My brave heart. My broken heart.

What I wished for never came true, nor could it. I could never return to the girl I was before. That girl was gone.

Some years ago, my mother and I went through boxes of old photographs together and came upon a picture of a young me. I was smiling broadly and happily into the camera with my head of messy curls thrown back. For an instant I caught sight of myself and felt my "used to be" spirit. My mother held the photograph and paused. She turned to me and said that it had been a long time since she had seen me like that.

Where did she go? She went down a road that took her far from home, from her sweetness and her innocence. She did things she could not change. She was changed by the things that she did.

in grey rain

I see you

emerge

running to find me

your certain smile

wide across your lovely face

a trace of light

envelops you

as you haste

and I wait

eager to learn

words you will utter

when I swing open the door

to let you in

begin

tell me

what I need to hear

on this day

when rain falls

cascading from heaven

onto my grief

give me reason

to believe

all is as it should be

or else I may die

from want of why

I chose this way

amazing grace

"When it rains," my grandmother used to say, "it means the angels are crying for someone." That day they wept for me. I know my grandmother was among them.

It was pouring, the kind of rain that drenches you in seconds. It just kept coming, streaming down and spilling off every surface and into every crevice, splashing up from feet, bouncing off umbrellas, spreading out into wide rivers down driveways and streets. The kind of rain that makes you wonder if it will ever stop and if Noah's ark was not such a farfetched idea after all.

I stood staring out the living room window, barely able to see the trees through the rain. The downpour shrouded the yard, the street and whatever lay beyond. As I watched, Sr. R emerged, running through the rain with a clutch of papers ineffectually held over her head in an effort to keep dry. She had left her office across the yard to make a dash for it. She was wearing her white dress with red flowers and wide belt; her appearance against the grey rain was striking. Without knowing, I knew she was coming to see me. I walked to the front door and swung it open.

Sr. R stood on the doorstep under the eaves, water dripping down her cheeks and arms. The wet wisps of auburn hair scattered about her freckled face made her even more lovely than usual. The sight of her at that moment is a memory I've relived countless times since that day. She smiled at me, trying to catch her breath, eager to say something. I didn't move or take my eyes from her as I waited for her to speak.

After a deep breath and a long exhalation, she found her voice and said, "There is Someone bigger than all of us in this!"

By "this" she meant my son, the adoption, his adoptive parents, me, all of it. I had signed the papers that morning giving him up. Forever. It was an act that required the separation of my heart from the conscious effort of my brain and the physical act of my hand moving the pen across the page. I chose not to think, not to hear, not to be there. If I had let myself feel, if conscious thought had entered my mind, I would have torn the adoption papers to shreds and run down the hallway to the nursery to claim my newborn son. Now I needed a sign that what I had done, what was now unchangeable, perhaps unforgivable, was right.

Sr. R brought me that sign. "There is Someone bigger than all of us in this," she repeated. "His parents chose the same name for him as you did. That has never happened before. It's a sign. From God." She beamed at me, happy to be the one delivering divine news.

With those words hanging in the air between us, she reached out and folded me into her arms. Like the rain gushing over the eaves, I let go. A deep sob, then tears. The agony I had suppressed was unleashed. Sr. R held me up, and I held on. I am not sure how long we stood there like that, but I recall a pause in time as the wet warmth of her buoyed me in my sorrow. I am usually a reluctant hugger, not really wanting to be touched, but when Sr. R held me, I fully embraced her. It would be the only comfort and love that I received that momentous day.

In those moments, I allowed myself to feel what I would deny for a long time after, in a futile effort to forget. Many years later I came across the term "broken open" in Elizabeth Lesser's book *Broken Open: How Difficult Times Can Help Us Grow*. I recognized myself in those words, but it took time and much reflection to reach the point at which I could learn from the relinquishment of my child. I kept what I felt tightly locked and hidden inside, not allowing anyone, including me, to see who I was or what I had experienced. Denial can be a strong motivator, but it is also a dark companion that sits in the corner and waits for you to acknowledge it. Denial is the bitter enemy that steals happiness and chokes bravery. It keeps you in its grip long past what you think you can abide.

Those moments in the doorway were the last I spent with Sr. R. When we finally unwound the tangle of arms, hurt and tears, she drew back to look at me. She asked me to never forget the sign I had been given. She urged me to have faith that things were as they were meant to be. She said. "As you return home to Newfoundland, carry with you the certainty that your choice for your son was guided by divine love."

Those words, divine love, have helped me through the inevitable regret. They are bigger than me. Forged of universal power, of which I am part of the whole. When I have woken from dreams where I hopelessly searched for my baby son, waking with the sheets wet from sweat and tears, I have sought comfort in her words. When I visited Halifax and searched the faces of every boy I met to find him, I had her words, like a mantra. When I needed fortitude to tell the story of my son to my children who came later, I prepared for that conversation with the memory of Sr. R standing in the doorway, shining like a light in the grey rain. I did not realize how much I would need her words and the memory of her lovely face as I made my way forward, day by day, into the long future.

People search for God, needing proof that he exists. I had a front-row seat: He showed up for me in the face and love of Sr. R. Until that moment in the rain, I thought God was either not real or just completely disinterested in me. In times of anger, I had cursed his name, believing that if he was out there, he had forgotten me. What kind of God could let me suffer those endless winter nights while I sat on the toilet pleading for mercy, begging to not be pregnant? He had been silent. Absent. Cruel.

"Forget God," I thought. "Religion is a lie."

Or so I believed until a Catholic nun emerged from the rain with the proof that God exists, even for me.

A few hours later I was sitting on the plane waiting for takeoff, bound for St. John's. It was still raining, coming down even harder and heavier. I pressed my cheek against the cool of the window beside me and closed my eyes, feeling oddly isolated in a plane full of chatty, busy passengers. Hot tears pushed through my eyelashes and slid down my cheeks. I turned away from the other passengers and let them come. I had come to Halifax with a baby in my womb. I was leaving without him.

"Let it rain, let the heavens open up and flood the world with the tears of heaven for my granddaughter," I could hear my grandmother shout.

"She is a child of God. And her son is God's gift just as his name proclaims."

I saw nothing of Halifax or Nova Scotia as we lifted off. I left that place in a storm of loss. It surrounded me, stayed with me and carried me home.

mine

not mine

mother

not mother

my life

PART III

AFTER LIFE

coming home

In the months that followed, I tried to re-establish my life and go on. Anyone looking at me saw a skinny twenty-two-year-old. I felt as though my skin was stretched over a cage and inside, I was a frightened little bird. I imagined that if someone scratched my surface, my secret would burst free to fly up in their face. It was a thin veneer, a fragile casing that with time and endurance would grow thick and sturdy as I learned to live with what I had done. But in the beginning, I was extremely vulnerable. I walked about waiting, even wishing, that someone or anyone would see through me and rescue me. My head and heart screamed for help while my tongue remained silent, my lips buttoned shut as I kept it all in.

On the night of my return, I saw Rob through the window at the gate as the plane taxied to the terminal. I had the urge to stay on the plane because getting off meant I had to face him. I wanted to be alone. Whatever he would say to me I did not want to hear. I thought I might just press my hands over my ears like a kid and scream, "lalalalalalalala-la!!!" What could possibly be an acceptable greeting? I was the girl he had pushed away to Halifax, by herself, to have the baby he did not want. The baby he would have preferred to abort for eight hundred dollars in some backstreet in New York City, even at the risk of me not making it out alive.

I slumped in my seat, hoping he would not see me even as I could not take my eyes off him, feeling something close to hate. He might have come to Halifax. But he had left me there alone to "deal" with the problem. Now that the problem was dealt with, I was coming home, and he was waiting at the airport as though I was arriving from a trip. The nasty business of my pregnancy out of the way, he was ready to greet me and be openly seen with me. But when I needed him most, he was nowhere to be found.

I did not want Rob that night. I wanted my mother. I always wanted my mother. I wanted the comfort of her. I wanted to cry into her soft shoulder and tell her how sorry I was that I was such a failure. I wanted to tell her what I had done. What I could not undo. I wanted to go home to my parents' house and climb into my old bed, stay there for days and see no one for a long, long time, maybe ever. I wanted to crumble under the weight of my decision, let it sink in. Be in a place where I could be safe. I had left my baby, my son, my beautiful boy behind in Halifax. I had signed adoption papers and given him to two people that I did not know. I wanted to crawl down in a deep dark place where no one could find me, and I wanted to stay there for as long as it would take for me to surface with some semblance of self-respect. Instead, I got off the plane and walked into the terminal.

I chose to be the sort of brave that sucks it up and goes on. What was the use of telling my mother after the fact? What if she hated me for giving up my son, her grandson? What if? What if? What the fuck if!?! No use going there.

I had a pact with that guy waiting in the terminal. I don't recall what he said to me. What I do remember is how he grabbed and held me. For a long time, we stood there with his arms wrapped tightly around me. There was a lot of feeling and emotion in his embrace. It seemed to be his way of telling me what he could not say out loud. That he was sorry? Relieved. Afraid. Grateful. Maybe he had worried up until the moment he saw me that I might have changed my mind and come walking off the plane with our son. Perhaps when I walked in, he recognized that I had been the one out there taking on the pregnancy and consequences by myself. Maybe seeing me made him realize what kind of nerve that required. Perhaps he was trying to make up for staying behind in Newfoundland. He might have sensed that I was changed, and felt he needed to pull me back to him to be sure of where he stood.

The marks on me were not visible, but they were there. Pregnancy altered my shape, my character and my heart. What I could not know before it happened was what adoption, giving up my child, would do to my soul. How it left me not quite knowing what had happened or why. It was a bitter choice, real and unreal. Nothing had ever hurt that much. Nothing does.

I looked at Rob knowing that I now had a place in me that he could not touch. Wisdom borne of pain, of doing something so far outside my life before it that I could never return to my original self. Perhaps that is what made him embrace me like he did. He was trying to get past something that was in his way.

I had made a choice. There was no second chance. Regret eats happiness and looks for more. Regret took hold and stayed, my devoted partner in a world where I now felt out of step and forever lost. Regret followed me into everything I did, a hefty burden that I hoisted onto my shoulders, day after day. I squinted out at the world unable to stand the light of people's happiness. I looked at everyone and felt less than them. Regret. It is with me still.

What I held inside was a dis-ease of the spirit. It led to a long disruption filled with doubt, uncertainty and jealousy. How could I possibly deserve love? How could I trust that anyone would love me and not turn away from me when someone shinier—happier and more whole—came along? I was a woman capable of giving up a child. Even if someone wanted to love me, I was unable to adequately love myself or anyone else. I pulled away from friends and family to protect myself, convinced I was protecting them too.

I've read, and I believe it to be true, that we must love ourselves before we can love and be loved by another. It took me many years to finally look in the mirror and say "I love you" out loud to the woman looking back at me. She stared back, smirked and noted how odd and unfamiliar it sounded to hear those words. She doubted. She hesitated. It took hearing the words repeatedly, spoken with growing conviction, to accept them. It felt peculiar. It felt like a betrayal of the young me, who declared that she loved her child more than herself and only that could justify what I had done. To love the me in the mirror shattered the one reality that made sense to me, that I was undeserving of love.

Years later, in the aftermath of my failed second marriage, I filled journals with dark anger and vicious poetry denouncing love. I wrote all the way back through my childhood to piece together who I was and how I became the story of pregnancy and adoption, "birth mother." I wrote and recorded my life until I found the strength to say, "Enough. Done. The time has come for forgiveness. Or else, there can be no life, no happiness, no freedom."

I left my second marriage to go in search of the me that I knew was possible. I failed twice at being a wife, even more often at life. I let down the two children I've had the privilege of raising more times than I can count. I was terribly unhappy and unmoored, drifting through my suburban life, trying to look like I belonged and cared. There was no amount of book clubs, PTA meetings or conversations over the fence with neighbours that could give me back my heart. I finally had to go claim my independence, my worth and myself as a woman. I had to end the struggle and commit to finding happy. I had to forgive what I held, in a tight fist of anger, as the most unforgivable act.

So often I have heard people start sentences with, "I could never bear ... I could not take ... I would not be able to stand ..." as they talk about things in life that they think are beyond them. Events of a magnitude they think would shatter them. I probably would have said the same had the unbearable not happened to me. I discovered I could endure far beyond what I had imagined.

It was this strength that finally took me back into my life, the ability to live without my first son. It gave me the ability to wake up every day and not go insane wondering if he was okay and if I had made the right decision. It is this strength that now lets me stare down all kinds of hurts and challenges without flinching. I have been in the clutches of my own version of the dragon and wrestled it to the ground. I walked away, hurt and broken in places, but walking. I have been in the arena where winning wasn't feasible, but surviving was, and I did.

I have lived through dark nights when the haunting cry of my son came across the miles and the years interrupting the silence to find me. What pain is greater than that? You can say anything to me. You can do anything to me. You can take all that I own. But you can never, ever hurt me the way the relinquishment of my child has hurt. There is nothing comparable. So, go ahead, tell me what you cannot handle. Then let me show my scars. I am undeterred and unaffected by your attempts to judge me, or worse, feel sorry for me. I am Beowulf staring down Grendel, sword in hand, with an intrepid heart. I am a fearless woman with wisdom born of experience and survival, striding my way into my earned hope and the certainty that out there I have a son who lives his life because of me.

What fear can daunt me? None. You too would be the same. In fact, you are. You just may not know it yet. But should the day come that you must fight, you will be able to do so. You will discover that what lies within you is fierce, relentless and powerful.

Initially, I chose adoption to save myself and Rob from public shame, a plan to get rid of a problem. No one would know. My reputation would be saved. Life would go on. It seems bizarre, looking back, that this was my greatest concern. The harsh judgement of others fended off, at all costs. It was more easily accomplished in the abstract than in fact—place baby for adoption.

Reality was quite different. Memories would not leave me alone. I went about my daily life, seemingly like any other person. Work and home and friends and things to do; I could be seen doing those normal things. I did them well. But inside me, there was what had happened, what I had done and now had to live with.

While I was in Halifax my physical experience of pregnancy became something lovely. As the baby grew, I felt his strong movements. I saw a bump poked out on the surface of my belly. A little foot, revealing the person who lived in me, with me, because of me. At night when I laid in my bed, he woke and stirred. I felt him. I loved him. During those nights as I lay quietly in the darkness, I was his mother, and he was my baby. I talked to him. Sang to him. Whispered sweet things to him. I wanted him to come into the world feeling wanted. I inscribed love on him in the hope that it would last his lifetime, that he would feel it even though I would not be with him.

He became very real in those last weeks of pregnancy. When I sang, he stirred, and I felt joy between us. We were on a shared journey, one in which he needed me, and I lived for him. His heart beat so close to mine, the beat, beat, beat of the rhythm of mother and child. Surely, he too felt my heart beat, beat, beating for him.

Love needs no logical explanation. It simply came into being, wrapping around my heart with an unseen but vivid force. It also destroyed the idea that I was giving up my child to protect my reputation, as Rob and I had agreed. In the end, whether my reputation was good or bad didn't matter. Love is what matters. It is the only thing that matters.

I gave up my child and will never, ever be able to undo that act.

Adoption is, in my estimation, an unnatural separation of mother and child. It leaves unintended scars that inevitably show up with time, for both. I have revisited my decision over and over, seeing it still as not right for me but right for my son. But while the outcome was likely right for him in large part, it could not banish the scars that come with being adopted and what it implies—not being wanted enough. It does not answer why. Nor does it explain why not.

"Why not keep me and make the best of things, knowing that love is most important?"

That's that hardest part. Knowing that love really might have been enough. That love could have made a way where the way had not yet appeared.

I
am the story
he
said not to tell
just as well
he's
long gone
so
whatever
I
say
is up to me now
and what
I
choose to reveal
will feel
good
to the bone
for
me
alone

used goods

It was one of the last things he said to me. I lugged it around with me, rejecting it, worrying it. I was leaving him. It was over. There was no going back, no recovering, no getting past the ugliness that had grown up between us. No amount of sorry could foster a change of heart.

As I stood with my suitcase at the door, he looked at me and said, "No one will want you. You are used goods."

I knew what he meant. It was not the sex part. It was the fact that I had a child that I gave up for adoption. A deal-breaker for someone who could not understand how I could do such a thing. While I was with Rob, it was our secret. Leaving meant that the secret would come along and be an issue for the next man who got close enough for me to tell him the truth.

As if hearing that would make take off my coat and boots and lift my suitcase back to the bedroom to unpack. Rehang my clothes in the closet. Put my underwear back in the drawer. And then wander back to the living room to resume my place in the chair beside him.

"Oh yes, you're right. I am used goods. I can't leave. What was I thinking? Now, where were we?"

But that is not what happened. I took those words along with my suitcase and walked out. I was done. Out the door was the unknown as well as my freedom. Out the door was my hope. I frankly did not give a damn if I was used goods. I had finally mustered the strength to leave. I did not think beyond that. I walked through the door and left, knowing it was what I had to do.

We stayed together for ten years after the adoption. I tried to remember our love as it had been before everything changed. It was the plan we made, the going on part after the adoption, that I somehow believed would eventually make everything make sense. I loved him, but I also hated him. I looked at him resentfully, vowing silently to myself that there would be no more children. He had doused that desire in me. I could never have another child with him, not after his rejection of the boy who now lived in the world separate from me.

No. Fucking. Way.

We went on. Not talking about our son. Not talking about what it did to us. But I knew it had done things to him. He carried a darkness from it. One night at a cabin where we had gone with friends for the weekend, I overheard him talking to his best friend. I had gone to bed and fallen asleep, while Rob stayed up to drink. It was long past midnight when I awoke to hear him tearfully telling the story of his younger sister who had had a baby. The sister who was my age and had been pregnant at the same time as me. No one knew about her pregnancy until the night she went into labour. She had planned to give up her baby too but chose to keep her.

It was a shock to hear this news that first night home. He'd related the story to me cautiously, assessing my reaction. I had a sense of falling and not being able to breathe.

That night in the cabin, as I listened from my bed in the darkness, he told his friend how he regretted not being kinder to his sister. He regretted not standing up for her. The family had essentially disowned her because of the baby, and he went along with it. I was certain that the pain and shame in his voice came from more than his sister. He did not reveal his own story, perhaps because of his pact with me. It might have been more than he could tolerate. But I heard it in his voice. I sensed it through the wall. I lay there listening. Wishing. Knowing that nothing could change what we had done.

We went on. Making a life and keeping the truth in a box for which the key had been lost. We lived together. But what needed to be said between us went unspoken; it festered.

In the summers he raced motocross, his passion. In winter he skied. I learned to ski, and we took ski vacations together with friends. On his bike or on the hill he was aggressive and fast. He did everything full on, no fear, no hesitation. I admired that trait in him. He was fit and strong and determined to be the best.

I spent my time running. I became pretty good at it and entered road races. I bought a twelve-speed bike that I rode to work and all over the city and beyond. I joined the Aquarena, a fitness club at Memorial University where I trained for a triathlon.

Running was my mainstay and my favourite. I ran year-round. I ran on snow and ice in the winter and when the weather was impossible, I ran on an indoor track at my fitness club. I ran through the hilly streets of St. John's. Up Hill O'Chips, up Signal Hill, up Prescott, up Cathedral, up Queen's Road. A lot of up. I ran around Quidi Vidi

Lake and through Quidi Vidi Village. I ran the length of Rennie's River Trail. I ran in and out of the quiet streets where tall maples sheltered Victorian homes in rustling arches of green on summer days. Running was my attempt at control. It was my way to have power over my body and my mind. When I was on the road with my feet carrying me, I was happy.

Over time, Rob and I developed parallel lives. He had his workout place and his friends, and I had mine. We moved into a house that his parents helped us purchase and set up a life. We painted and decorated, making it a home, at least in appearance. After work, he went to his gym and I went to mine. I would arrange to be home first so that I could have the evening meal ready when he came in, as he expected. I stood watching for his car, so I could quickly go downstairs and have his dinner at the table as he walked through the door. I hated myself for being like that. It demoralized me. It made me hate him too. I wanted us to work out together and make food together. Yet, I never pushed for that. I left it alone in favour of keeping the peace.

My career as a registrar at the Marine Institute was going well, and I was gaining respect as a leader in post-secondary education. I enjoyed working with people and developing a team. I put my heart into my work. I was in my office early and stayed late. Having my own office, staff and substantial responsibility motivated me to succeed. I put aside my dream of being a professor and a writer to take up a career of leadership, students and making a difference in the lives of others. We implemented technology solutions. We eliminated the typewriter and multipart forms to move into the information age. We focused on the student experience as a crucial part of college success. And there I was, an English major, stepping into the "brave new world" that previously had only been in books for me.

It could have been a happy life for us. There were elements of love still between us. From the outside looking in, it may have been possible to assume happiness and love. Yet up close, privately, the issues felt insurmountable.

He asked me to marry him. I had come home from a conference late one night and in the morning, I woke up to find him already out of bed and downstairs in the kitchen. As I walked in to make breakfast, he stood there waiting for me. He held out a ring and proposed. Just like that. I don't remember the words he said or how I responded but the answer was yes and then he hugged me. It was not the most romantic of proposals. I stood there in his arms feeling apprehensive. Maybe even disappointed. I did not feel the yes that had come out of my mouth. I wanted it to be romantic, not a before-breakfast question. "Pass the coffee, here's your toast and oh, by the way, will you marry me?" But I wonder now if I needed his proposal—and a wedding—to finally convince myself that I was lovable. "He may not have loved me enough then to marry me and help provide a home for our baby," some part of me said, "but I have made him love me that much now."

We kept the engagement to ourselves. We decided to plan and arrange the wedding quickly, a quiet elopement ceremony with two friends as witnesses. My best friend was married to an Anglican minister who agreed to marry us in the chapel located on Memorial University's campus. He met with us briefly prior to the wedding in lieu of the usual marriage preparation course. We were both relieved not to endure a course in which we would have been assessed for suitability to be a married couple. The minister revealed to my friend after that he'd noted a reluctance in me that he later wished he'd explored.

He was not the only one. A close friend, the only one who knew about our engagement and wedding plans, took me to lunch. She candidly asked me why I was getting married. I had not thought about why until she said it. "I think things will get better once we are married," I responded. She said that marriage would not repair what was wrong or replace what was missing. I held firm on my notion that, because he asked me to marry him, it meant that he loved me. That was what I had always wanted. To be loved by him.

Of course, the problem was not on his side. The problem was on mine. With me. I felt it in my bones when he held me after I said yes. I did not want his arms around me. I stood there with the urge to push him away. I did not want him to touch me. That's not the kind of reaction an engagement ring, love and marriage should generate.

I married him anyway. We said "I do" and then celebrated over dinner with our friends at the Hotel Newfoundland. We had reserved a honeymoon suite and had our first night as husband and wife overlooking the harbour and downtown St. John's. The wedding was simple but not without charm. The meal, the room and the city were lovely. On that, our wedding night, I had a sense of hope and promise. But marriage is not a ceremony and it is not a honeymoon. It is the everydayness of waking up with the same person, living in the same house, paying bills and taking care of gardening, cleaning and cooking. It is ordinary life enhanced with love and intimacy, passion and kindness. Adoration and joy. I had lost those feelings in Halifax and could not find them anymore. I could not undo my resentment of him any more than I could undo the adoption. I just kept trying to make something good out of something bad.

Our honeymoon was a trip to Costa Rica with Rob's family, minus the sister they'd disowned. I did not want a honeymoon that included his parents and siblings, and we argued on the trip. One night he was so angry he threatened to push me down a bank, telling me that there were snakes and other creepy creatures waiting for me down there. I taunted him back: "Go ahead. Push me."

Sitting at the pool, lying on the beach, I thought of his vicious attacks and my angry retorts. I looked at him next to me, serene and relaxed, unable to reconcile the man that he was in anger with the man he became in moments of calm. The trip was a bleak forecast for our marriage.

We flew back from Costa Rica through Boston, where we had a layover. We spent the night in an upscale hotel, a relief from our rustic accommodations in Costa Rica. I was tired of cockroaches, wild boars and reptiles. One morning, an iguana had poked its head in through the thatched roof above me as I stood in the shower and I nearly collapsed from fright. I called for assistance and a houseboy showed up with a broom and told me in broken English, "Next time you see iguana. Take broom. Go like this." (He demonstrated by hitting the ceiling with the end of the broom.) "Iguana go bye-bye." After that, I took quick showers and spent as much time as possible out of the room.

In Boston, I was glad to be in a room with fluffy white towels, thick soft pillows and bedding—and the guaranteed absence of critters of any kind. I took a leisurely shower and slept like the dead.

That was our marriage. Huge swings between calm and crazy.

Going from all is well to all hell breaking loose. He yelled. I yelled. I cried. He mocked. Then there was silence. And in that silence a resumption of life in the absence of anger until it reappeared and took hold of us once more. I tried to manage his anger with strategies such as my carefully orchestrated timing of meals. I anticipated his needs and met them, a dangerous solution that left me stockpiling unaddressed, unresolved resentments.

We were married less than nine months. We tried. We both tried. But in the end, it was clear that it had been over for ten years. The time had come to make a choice for myself. To some people, it may have looked cruel for me to leave him when I did, at a time he wanted and needed me more than ever. But I did not leave him because I was heartless. I left him because my heart was broken.

In May 2011, I flew from Arizona to Newfoundland to be with my oldest brother, who was dying from cancer. I was hurriedly packing my suitcase when Rob suddenly came to mind.

The daring I'd admired in him had led to tragedy. As our marriage disintegrated in 1993, he'd had a motocross accident that left him paralyzed and in a wheelchair. Now I had a vision of him wheeling in the door at St. John's airport and coming up to me, smiling, to say hello. In the many times I had travelled through St. John's since we divorced, I had not once run into him. I brushed the thought aside and finished packing.

The next night that vision played out as I had imagined it. He wheeled through the door and came up to me to say hello, his big smile the same as I had known it years before. I told him why I was travelling home, and we spoke for a few minutes about my brother, who Rob had known well and liked. Rob was meeting his wife, who had been on my flight. Before he left me, he said there was something he had wanted to tell me. He said that his sister, the one who had been disowned for keeping her baby, had died of cancer, but that before she did, Rob had "made things right with her." He seemed relieved and pleased to tell me. I looked into the blue eyes that had first drawn me to him so long ago in our political science class. I held his gaze for a moment, grateful to hear what he was telling me.

We parted, and I left to meet my sister and brother, who were flying in from Ontario. I could not wait to tell them what had happened and how I had envisioned it the night before. Talking about Rob's sister brought me back to that night in the cabin and his confession to his friend. For the first time, I understood the depth of the hurt in Rob, the pain he had carried for a long time. It was good that he had made it right with his sister. It makes me hopeful that one day he will get to meet our son. Maybe along with me. Maybe because of this book. We cannot change the past, but we can do better now, and going forward. That night in the airport gave me considerable comfort. When he moved away from me, he kept looking back, smiling. It was meant to happen.

Forgiveness did not come all at once. It came in pieces. A scattered collection of moments, insights and wisdom gathered over time, until my heart softened, allowing me to see more than my own perspective. I could spend the rest of my life blaming and resenting him. "What he did to me" on my lips as proof that I was the one hurt and mistreated.

Yes, he was abusive and sometimes cruel. Those things were a part of us, but they were not all of us. How he acted, what he did, are as connected to who he was and what he struggled with, as they are to me. That he had reached out to his sister and wanted me to know said a lot about what he'd experienced.

We gave up our son. And then we suffered the consequences. His anger. My resentment. They were the savage outcomes that got in between us and tore us apart as we blamed one another without being able to articulate why. Just as I looked at him as the cause of my pain and loss, he must have looked at me as the source of his.

That night in the airport was the final piece of forgiveness. I was finally able to fully let go of the past and its hold on me. I looked at him and was thankful to be in his presence having this brief, long-awaited conversation. I saw him not as the one who wronged me, but as the one who shared one of life's most profound and far-reaching consequences with me. I saw him as the first man who ever loved me and realized that it came undone because of the choice we'd made, first to save us from shame and rejection by others, then, for me, at least, because it seemed the most loving thing to do. We endured the consequences separately, unwilling and unable to talk about it. After, I stayed with him in the ashes of our love until leaving was the only way to save myself.

He said to me once, after I left him, that we made a mistake, that we should have kept our son. I did not want to hear it at the time. Now I see it as his attempt to say that he too was sorry. What might we say today if we sat across from one another, stronger, wiser—perhaps ready to tell the whole story? This is how I know I have forgiven him. I ask such questions and their answers would be welcome. Surely, he has tangled with our secret through sleepless nights and random moments of sorrow. Surely, he knows the shape of regret and the torment of no way back. It is there, always there, waiting to snatch us from now and send us back into the past.

last night
I dreamed you here
with me
we spoke of things
as though
we were familiar
you looked at me
as though
I was your mother
today
I stay
inside the dream
because it seems
more real
than not

now

Thirty-five years have gone by. I am in awe of that. Thirty-five years—420 months, 12,775 days. A lot of time. Each day lived moment by moment until here I am looking back wondering how it can be that thirty-five years have gone by since my son was born. I looked out to the future in 1983 with unseeing eyes and an unknowing heart. What would come, how I would feel and how I would change were indiscernible. It is best not to know what lies ahead. What is best, what has been best for me, is to go forward with the belief that I can control many things but that surprises, good or bad, influence me, and that the things I cannot control are that way for a reason.

My son is a man now. I try to see him as a man yet in my eyes he is still the little baby boy that I kissed tenderly as he lay sleeping in the hospital nursery. I can close my eyes at any time and still recall his scent, the soft silkiness of his new skin, and his quiet movements as he squirmed in his sleep. Those moments are my sole connection with him, and I have relived them so often, the memory of my child. I feel him in that memory. I gave him my heart, my love, and everything that I desired him to know as a mother, imprinting herself upon her son. In those few moments, we were mother and son.

Over the years I have read from a substantial list of self-help books. Books about how to improve my thinking. Books on how to be positive. How to be happy. Books on how to live more fully, more honestly, more authentically. Books on how to be successful, financially secure, and have everything you want in life. Books on leadership and courage and taking risks. Books on how to overcome obstacles, face fear, understand weaknesses. Books on how to be a good mother. Each of those books and countless Oprah shows and magazines were devoured as I attempted to address what I thought was wrong with me, what I lacked.

Based on the ever-growing number of self-help and inspirational books in every bookstore, I am not unlike a lot of people. Every time I purchased one of those books, I went home certain that the answers I needed would be inside the covers. Answers to questions not even fully formed in my mind but felt deep within me. I still get that same thrill, like a drug dose, each time I come upon a book title that promises to "fix" me. Just holding the book ignites hope. I can stand in the self-help section of a bookstore and almost hear the voices calling to me from these books.

"Pick me! I've got what you need."

I admit this at the real risk of sounding off balance. But I have on numerous occasions set down money for a book hoping its contents might free me. Seeking the magic formula, the golden ticket to happiness. Longing for the way out of pain, disappointment and self-ridicule.

It's not that I wanted an external, paid-for solution. I was willing to, and did, considerable work on my inner self through these books. I took directions, completed the exercises, did whatever the book of the day said was necessary to improve myself. And there was a lot of valid, useful advice. I learned a lot. But I have yet to discover the book that explains how to get over giving up a child for adoption. I imagine titles for such books, but I have never found them.

Ten Steps to Recovery after You Sign the Adoption Papers
– guaranteed to work or your money back!

Adoption: What Every Birth Mother Needs to Know

The Seven Habits of Highly Effective Birth Mothers

*What They Don't Tell You about Giving Up
a Child for Adoption Unveiled*

Not a likely list of titles, but I guarantee you I would have picked them up, read the jackets inside and out, skimmed the chapters, and taken them home. I would have stayed up late into the night searching for answers.

My mother said I needed God. But I felt like a fraud in church. "God sees all. God knows all. He knows your sins." It's hard to pray and sing about God's love and forgiveness when you are living a lie, keeping a dark secret. God may have been waiting for me to admit the error of my ways so I could be saved, find forgiveness and absolution. The problem was that I considered my sin unforgivable, maybe not by God, but surely by all those righteous church members. But whose forgiveness did I really need anyway? Not those who judged me and not even God. Forgiving myself was what I needed most.

Over the years, I've attended my parents' church in our hometown and found myself surrounded by women who kept their babies born outside of marriage, raised up by the community. Young pregnant girls who were supported and taken in by their family. Once the tut-tutting and crying were done, the pregnancies were accepted, and the babies lived in love and acceptance. Everyone made the best of things and life went on. I sat among them considering what my life might have been had I taken the family and community route. I sat among them knowing I was not like them. I did not have their brand of resilience.

Of course, most of the perceptions about how I might have been judged were my own. Without revealing my secret to anyone, in or out of church, I was left to torture myself with possibilities. I would slide into the pew and fake my way through the rituals and sermon and hymns. I was the black sheep they did not recognize. I might have been cast out and shunned if they knew. Or I might have been redeemed, but on their terms. I sometimes considered the second option but dismissed it quickly. Even if people were nice to my face, the phone calls and gossip certain to happen behind my back were more than I could tolerate.

"She's a tramp after all."

"She thought she was something but she's just like the rest of us. Worse. She gave up her baby to save herself and now she's back here looking for sympathy. Not likely."

"Serves her right."

"Oh, how the mighty have fallen."

That's what I imagined them saying because I had heard as much about other girls.

My mother wondered why I resisted going to church. She encouraged church almost as much as she encouraged school and education. She was absolute in her belief that it was essential for a good life.

I am not agnostic or an atheist. I have my own spiritual beliefs. I choose to think of God as a universal source of light, love and energy of which I am one part of the greater wise and infinite whole. God is not punitive. He does not keep a scorecard or checklist or offer a confessional option. And if I am telling my story, and I am, God is not a "he." It bothered me that the holy trinity was the father, son and the holy ghost. I could not see myself in that.

Church was a male-dominant source of angst for me. Man-made rules and interpretations of the Bible left me on the outside—conform and be forgiven. I wanted a source of spirituality that would accept me, flaws and all. What I was carrying was not one confession away from forgiveness. It was a part of me. I went in search of a way to cope, survive and live with myself.

pour me a coffee

and come

sit with me

as we gaze

out the window

to the street

and the trees

and the people

we see

passing by

unaware

of our stare

as I tell you

my story

while the tears

of my glory

drip

into my cup

family matters

Another snowfall had arrived overnight and glistened bright in the morning sun. It was New Year's Day, 2014. My brother suggested a walk in the woods with his young dog Sophie and I readily agreed, glad to work off the endless holiday sweets and long days lounging on the couch. Cold, fresh air and brilliant sun reflecting off pure white snow greeted us. Sophie bounded ahead, eager to get on the trail and run. I focused on her black fur as my eyes tried to adjust to the sunlight. My brother and I ambled behind her, unable to keep her pace but anxious not to lose sight of her in case snowmobiles came quickly around a corner. Sophie raced up and down the inclines of the trail as we climbed out of the neighbourhood. She dug her head into the soft snow, pulling up excitedly to show her powdery white snout and ears. She made us laugh and then almost fall over as she ran between our legs with the kind of energy only a puppy can muster.

As we came to the crest of the trail, the view opened up under the clear blue sky. Trees lined up like dancers in draped white dresses, elegant and beautifully poised. From where we were, the land was entirely peaceful. Silence rang in our ears, making our breath and every word we spoke crisp in contrast. Except for Sophie, everything was still and cathedral quiet. Under the sun and the weight of wool and down I felt warm. A trickle of sweat crept down my spine to the small of my back. These woods were not unfamiliar to me, but I did not know them like my brother, who called out the names of the trails and ponds as we came upon them. This was his backyard, one that stretched out in many directions and that he had travelled many times.

It was here he found the moment to speak to me about the adoption. It may not seem an unusual thing for a brother to talk to his sister about a secret revealed after thirty years except that it is not something that the men in my family have easily done. Maybe this is true of other families, as it is in mine, that the women do the talking, and then tell the men. It may be that within their marriages the men say what they think, but neither my father nor my brothers spoke much to me about the difficult parts of my life. The day my brother spoke of his sadness and regret for all that I had borne alone was a rare occurrence.

I never found the nerve to begin the conversation with my father. I might have witnessed disappointment, or worse, tears in his eyes, and that would have been too difficult. I heard instead through my mother how it saddened him that I lived with pain and loss. The closest my father came to the subject was when he said he considered me the strong one in our family. Much of what I know about my father's feelings for me were in those words. I understood he meant I could get through things where others would not have. But he also meant that I had to be strong, that it was required of me, to endure a life without my child. Strong meant living with both courage and fear along a sliding scale of intensity, depending on the day or state of mind.

There are moments when the love of a family member is a salve that heals the hurt spaces no one else can reach. It washes over you and fills in the crevices that have been empty and aching. That is what my brother's words to me were on that morning. I could not tell him how much it meant to me because my emotions would have tumbled out in waves, surprising him and embarrassing me. He did not dwell on the subject for long. He spoke of it with an honest, heartfelt concern and remarked on how I must have suffered through the years that I had kept the secret. We did not stop walking. There were no hugs or tears. We spoke of it and then moved on to other things. Yet, I was comforted and relieved. Speaking of the adoption with my brother liberated me from worry that had been present for me at every family gathering.

I had planned to tell my story to my oldest brother, but I never got to fulfill that wish. Before he died in 2011, the plan had been for me to spend two weeks at home, just the two of us talking and being together. But the call came from my mother to move up my flights and get there as soon as possible. He'd gone into a coma and there was no hope that he would revive. His cancer had been swift and merciless.

I had been writing and putting together music to share with him. I intended to tell him about the real me, what I had gone through and how I had survived. I wanted to tell him what I could not say to our father. I envisioned the two of us talking for hours. I believed that if I told him my story then I would be able to tell everyone else. But most of all, I wanted to tell him before he died.

When I arrived, he was in the final hours of his life. I walked into the hospital room to see him lying curled on the bed, a small, gaunt version of my brother. His breathing was laboured. He was with us but not with us. I was shocked to see that he was so far gone. I knew in an instant that everything I had written and prepared to tell him would remain unspoken. I had lost the opportunity. I looked around at my family and before I could stop myself, I demanded to know why they had left it so long to call me home. It was unfair of me to say this, yet they responded kindly that they'd had no real warning. All signs had pointed to him doing better. Then it went completely the other way.

There are aspects to my brother's passing that I hesitate to tell as they may seem contrived. But I tell them anyway because they heal my heart and they were real for me. My brother waited for me, for all of us who flew from some distance to be with him in those final hours. I knew it. He stayed alive because he meant for us to have time together. He waited.

As his life grew shorter, measured into minutes, a special gift was offered to me. My brother's best friend asked if I wanted some time alone with my brother. He said he knew I had written some things to share with him. I don't know how he knew that, but I eagerly took the offer. Once everyone was out of room, I was alone with my brother in the quiet; the only sounds were his breath and my heartbeat. I sat with my iPad on my lap and my right hand over his left hand. I read the beginning of the things I needed to say to him. I came to the end of the page. His hand moved, and his head turned towards me. I stopped. Without a word spoken, he seemed to tell me not to worry. He already knew everything I was going to say.

I put my iPad aside and sat with him then for a few moments. He had been the one in the family who knew me best. He could catch my eye across a room, nod and smile as he leaned into his guitar to sing and I would see how he loved me. Much of the love he carried for me went unspoken. Yet he could come up behind me and lay a hand on my shoulder and I'd feel it. He looked out for me, desired better for me. When I was a little girl, he would come home from trips away with presents. In the 1960s, little girls loved bride dolls and I still have the one he brought home from a trip just for me. She became a funny reminder of my failed marriages and of never having had a wedding dress. She has long since lost her flowers and veil, but she still wears her silky underpants and her white high-heel sandals. (Best of all, I loved the red painted nails on her fingers and toes.) I was drawn to that kind of glamour even as a small girl. I would steal shoes from visiting aunts and prance into the midst of my mother's entertainment, horrifying her that I could be so bold. Pretty shoes on my feet made me happy and I found them irresistible. I took the scolding for the sake of a few minutes of wearing forbidden heels.

I was destined to be all girl and my brother saw that in me. We shared a loved of clothes that made walking out into the world an event. He had a fabulous green leather jacket that reminded me of James Dean. Sexy, confident and a little mysterious. My brother was devastatingly handsome when he lit a cigarette and sang into a microphone as though nothing on earth mattered more to him, save his wife and family. His guitar, his voice and the white spiral of smoke from a cigarette beside him are etched in my memory. It was those damn cigarettes that took him in the end but for all those years, when he strapped on a guitar and made us glad to be in his presence, it seemed like nothing could be better than listening to him sing. I think now that if I asked him what mattered, he'd smile that sideways grin and say that to have lived well is far better than to have lived long. I am inclined to agree.

He knew me, and in his dying moments he told me so. I looked at him, the silence growing more pronounced as his breathing slowed to a whisper. His head turned towards me and I felt his hand move in mine. I sensed him telling me that he needed to go. I stood up from my chair, kissed my brother on his forehead and left to find my family. I opened the door, and as if I had called them, there they stood all together in the hallway with my small mother in the middle, surrounded by the others. "It's time," came out of my mouth and they flooded into the room with me. My nephew played his guitar as we sang my brother up to heaven with the song "You Are My Sunshine." It was a sad, sweet salute and farewell to the eldest in our family.

I had never witnessed a person die. In those last moments with him, I experienced the arrival of peace. One slow breath after another, as death quietly took him from his body into the spirit world beyond. He was love in those moments, the purest kind of love, love that has been released from the physical and set free. The wonder of it was not that I felt him leave but that I felt him stay. I cannot quite describe it, but I know for certain that death is not an ending. There is more. It has been said that between life and death there is a thin veil. If that is true, I like to think that my brother remains close.

I miss him still. The sound of him. His music. His way of pleasing my mother by just walking through her door and sliding in beside her on the couch. I miss how he loved Christmas and would do anything to make the season fun and memorable, like going up on the roof with sleigh bells to convince me that Santa Claus was real. I hid my head under the covers wanting to believe in Santa, but knowing it was really my brother and adoring him for being so great. I miss going to his cabin on the pond where he cleared land and built his little piece of heaven on earth. I miss watching him sing and encouraging others to join in. I miss how he loved family, all of us. He was the eldest in our family, a place of honour he fulfilled just by being himself.

When I learned he was dying, I worried about what I would say to comfort him. Yet when I called, it was him that comforted me. He said, "There is a time to live and a time to die. If it's my time to die, I am ready to go. I have had a good life." He only cried when I said that I was taking two weeks to come visit him so that we could have time together. It meant a lot to him. He knew it would be the last time he would see me, and it was time that we wished we had had more of over the years.

It was as I sat beside his grave that it came to me to write my story and share it, first and foremost with my son. I might spend a lifetime waiting and hesitating, only to find it's too late and the opportunity lost. Death is the exit point. My brother's life taught me that if you do what matters, then whenever the end comes you are ready to go, without regrets.

we are mothers you and I
of a different sort
we had children long before
we had a life
back when we were young and easy
we chose to give them up
and let them call another mother
chose for them a separate life
from us
we hid our pain
walked on into the future
not forgetting
silently remembering
behind our smiling faces
there was a story
needing to be told
long kept secrets coming loose
untangling from guarded memories
your story and mine
mothers sharing
what it means to have a child
to love that child
to let the child go
and never know
if life will ever bring them home

we are mothers you and I
of a different sort
I know your story
and you know mine

birth mothers

Whenever I've told my story, there are so many birth mothers who come forward to call it their own. Like me, they know what it means to live a secret. I have come upon these women in many different circumstances. We find each other not by seeking but by knowing. We see it in each other's eyes; we recognize that we are one and the same through the choice we have in common. I have been in living rooms with other birth mothers and over the course of an evening we reveal and bond through our stories. I have accidentally heard women talking and soon found that I was in the group, speaking with them, because they mentioned the word adoption. I have told my story in public settings and was quickly surrounded by women who said they too had placed a child for adoption, or had had an abortion, or wanted to know how I survived.

Some women were forced as young girls to give up their child to spare their family shame and community rejection. Some women were raped and could not bear to keep a child conceived in violence. Some, like me, had a boyfriend who insisted that there be an abortion or an adoption. Some were too young to know what to do. Each one of us

353

struggled to decide. Not one of us has ever been relieved of the consequences of our decision.

In 1998, journalist and long-time television host Anne Petrie wrote and published her book *Gone to An Aunt's: Remembering Canada's Homes for Unwed Mothers*. I read it along with some of my birth mother friends. The book validated my experience of living in a home for unwed mothers. It also depicted the elements of shame and secrecy that largely influenced my path in 1983. Unwed mothers were still outcasts in those days. We were held accountable for our "sins" and loose ways. Rob and I were under the spell of those social judgements. He was afraid of what his family and friends would think. I was afraid of my hometown and being a failure in the eyes of those who knew me. The need for social approval and the proper order of dating, love, marriage and children stayed at the forefront as we chose to cover up our "mistake" and conceal the truth.

Birth mothers make a hard choice when they give up a child for adoption. They choose to give their child the life that they cannot provide, the life that will protect them. There are many reasons and circumstances. Sometimes the decision is primarily about the birth mother and her well-being. Sometimes it is for both the mother and the child.

Less examined and even less understood is that, when birth mothers release their child into the care of others, they do not release themselves from the pain and regret of living without their child. I have yet to meet a birth mother who says that she is at peace with her choice.

Birth mothers forever worry that we will be harshly judged. After all, we question *ourselves* about how it was possible for us to do what we did. Surely, others think the same. Many of us have later had more children, which raises the question of how we could give up one child but go on to have others. In my experience, the emotional complexity of adoption was a shadow over the mother I was to the children I raised. The hurt of the lost child has been a constant background and one that frequently undid me. It was the secret that I had to share with my children when I thought they were old enough to understand. It is always present in my relationship with them, yet rarely discussed. They have a brother they will likely never know. They have a mother who gave him up and who wears her regret in front of them.

I ask other birth mothers how they cope. Through tears, they tell me that it has been difficult and sad and overshadowed by regret. They cannot forget their children and they cannot stop hoping for them to show up. They say that if it were possible, they would have changed their decision many times over. I know that feeling. It chases me. It finds me in my sleep where I go back in time to that very moment of signing the adoption papers and I tear them up. The dreams are not kind. In some, I am searching for my son, up and down the hallways of hospitals and the adoption agency but I cannot find him. People are mocking me and telling me to go home. It is a scar so deep it never heals.

As birth mothers, we know that we could have kept our babies. We could have been single moms. We understand that, with hindsight and maturity. I have unyielding respect for those who chose to be single mothers. Their stories shed light on the plight of women who face the odds and do what they must to create a home and life with their child. Theirs are the stories of young girls who sucked it up and lived with their parents until they could make it on their own, stories of love from an angle that I will never know. I used to consider single mothers a better version of the unwed than me. But these days I choose to consider them a different version. I cannot tell their story, but I empathize with them and appreciate what it took to be that kind of brave. I see single mothers every day. Carrying on. Succeeding. Thriving.

The birth mother looks like everyone else. She can be your friend, your workmate, your sister—you would never know that she is a birth mother unless she told you. And the telling is damn hard. I recall the summer afternoon, standing in my brother's cabin in Newfoundland with my brothers and sisters-in-law, the words forming in my mouth to tell them. I tried and hesitated, tried and hesitated. The moment passed. I lost my will to speak. The afternoon wore on. As we gathered around the table to eat supper, I felt silent relief. Or was that regret? The loss of what might have lovingly unfolded had I found the strength to open up? It was easier to not speak, to remain silent, to keep the secret.

As the years stacked up, I grew used to my secret; protective of it. I could bear it alone, but I did not know if I could endure what other people would say or do. I did not know if I could handle their questions as they sought to understand my actions. I had drawn my strength from surviving. There was nothing that I could not face. I did not require support or compassion. I sure as hell did not want pity and I could not stand judgement. I was harsh on myself. I have stood in front of my mirror and hated the woman looking back at me. I let that woman in the mirror suffer relationships that were no good. I lived for years believing I did not deserve happiness because of what I had done.

No one, not a single person, could be permitted to land further judgement on me. It might, I thought, be the thing that broke me.

Somehow, though, the time comes for birth mothers to unpack our stories from their secret quarters. We pull them out cautiously and share them sparingly. We let you see us as we are, with considerable trepidation. It is then that we realize that the hiding was worse. We welcome love into our hurt and, while it cannot fully heal us, it repairs our self-esteem. We learn to trust that others will not judge because they and everyone, all humans, wear scars. We all have stories we have not told and need to tell. Telling is the way out.

I feared telling my mother more than anyone else. She found out by accident. I was at home seeking the comfort of my parents at the end of my short marriage. As is my practice, I was writing down my feelings on a mountain of loose-leaf pages. A messy testimonial to my heartache. I left them on my bed to go take a shower. When I came back, my mom was in my bedroom. She had gone in there to put laundry away and came upon my writing. She stood in front of me with the pages in her hands.

She said first that she did not know what provoked her to pick up the pages and start reading but something told her she was meant to read what I had written. And she did. The next thing she said was, "What have you done?"

We sat there unable to move. Silent. I could feel her breathing, the warmth of her so close to me. I could almost hear her heartbeat. The house was silent too as if it paused with us, holding its breath, waiting for us to speak, to move. Somewhere outside my father was working in the yard, going about his tasks oblivious to what was now happening inside his house,

I looked at her hands. The hands that raised me from child to woman. Honest, kind hands that worked hard each day to make life good. Preparing food. Washing dishes. Hanging laundry on the clothesline in summer's sunny breezes and winter's bitter cold. I can see her still, coming through the door at the end of summer day with her basket overflowing with clothes that smelled of sunshine and fresh air. She'd stand at the end of the couch folding each item, talking to us while we breathed in the scent of that laundry, pleased with her efforts, her satisfaction obvious.

In winter, she would come through the door with frozen-stiff shirts and pants that made me laugh because they looked like men and ladies without their heads, hands and feet. She'd carry her rigid bundles to the basement and pin them on a line that ran near the wood stove my father had installed down there for winter comfort. She hummed and sang, not seeming at all perturbed by the double duty of two clotheslines. When I asked her why she bothered to hang clothes outside in winter when they would not dry but only freeze, she just looked at me puzzled and replied that there was nothing better than that cold fresh air to make clothes smell good.

My mother's energy and enthusiasm for household chores impressed me but did not pass on to me. She rose to her work with unfailing love and purpose that made our home a nest to curl up in and delight in its simple pleasures. My mother moved about her house with grace and happiness, her whole world captured in small joys. She was a mom with an apron tied about her waist, elbow deep in dough. It was an artistry of flour, salt, water and yeast kneaded and transformed into golden loaves.

Her hands rarely took a rest. When she needed downtime, she was most likely to watch *Days of Our Lives* while she sat knitting. Her version of a break, her daily meditation, was row upon row of stitches. It is impossible to think of my mother and not think of her knitting. She said that it was what long winter evenings were good for, whiling away the hours over patterns and projects.

The first sweater I recall my mother making me was a thick woollen red cardigan with a skater on the back. I so loved that sweater and thought it magic how she made the picture of the skater appear. I wore it when I went skating on the frozen cove near our house. I fell countless times, trying to be the kind of skater that my sweater inspired. At the end of skating, I walked up the hill, up the lane, with my skates hung over my shoulder, my frosted fingers and toes already warming at the certainty of hot chocolate in my mother's kitchen. She'd give me warm woollen socks and a mug of steaming hot cocoa as I pulled up a chair to be close to the kitchen stove. The yellow glow of our little house, the smell of dinner to come and my mother close by made me a happy little soul.

It was my mother's hand that I first held when walking out the door into the world. We went hand in hand to the corner store. She pressed a dime into my palm and folded my fingers overtop, coaxing me not to lose it on the way. I held it tightly as we walked, the dime in one hand while my other hand rested inside my mother's, tethering me to her protection and certainty.

A dime could buy a couple of things in the 1960s. A bar of chocolate and potato chips, for instance. Sometimes I got both. Sometimes I got one and saved a nickel for my piggy bank. If it was summer, I got ice cream. A Dixie Cup with a little wooden spoon inside the cover.

My mother might buy bologna and cheddar cheese, the cheese cut from a large wheel that sat atop a counter I could hardly reach. The store owner would cut a generous wedge, according to my mother's instructions, and then place it on the shiny white and silver scale to determine the price. Each time, he winked at me and handed me a small edge of cheese to nibble while he served my mother. The bologna and cheese would be wrapped in brown paper and tied with cotton string, perfect small packages to carry home. As we made our way back, I'd skip along beside my mother, anxious to get home and enjoy my treat.

There is a photograph of my mother and me taken on a day we went to a garden party, a summer tradition in Newfoundland in the 1960s. My mother is standing beside me; I am seated on my swing in our front yard. She is wearing a sleeveless dress, white with a flower print and a wide belt, cinched and flared from the waist. My dress is blue, and I wear a white hat with a ribbon. On my feet are my Sunday best socks and shoes. My mother is young and stylish, carefully and tastefully dressed for the occasion. I am small, maybe four, with ringlets falling out from underneath my hat.

It may be that my memory of that day is more the photograph than anything else. Whatever is true or imagined, I maintain it left me with an abiding connection to the feminine strength that was my mother. I found in her the loveliness of being a woman. The pleasure of wearing a beautiful dress was a love she and I had in common, one that could take us outside the ordinary into an expression of our best selves.

Long after the day we sat together on the bed, breathing uncertainly into our shared space and sorrow, my mother said something to me that remains a great gift of my life. It came after I had survived two failed marriages and the heartache of trying but not finding love. It came after I had driven out of the Arizona desert and wound my way north to a new life in Vancouver, after I found the courage to reinvent my life. It came after I stood on my own two feet and took charge of my future. It came after all that, after feeling like I had repeatedly disappointed my mother and had failed to be a good daughter. Unexpectedly, one night as we spoke on the phone, me in Vancouver and her in Newfoundland, she said that she thought I was the version of her she might have been if she had had my education and opportunities. In that moment, I realized that she chose to see me not as my mistakes but as a woman whose strength and wisdom she admired.

I told my mother that day that it was because of her that I was strong, that I got up every day and went to school and developed a lifelong love of learning. It was because of her that I reached beyond my small town and followed my dream to university. It was because of her that I never gave up no matter what happened. It was because of her, that day as we sat side by side on my bed with the first pages of my story falling down around us, that I finally chose to begin to believe myself worthy of love. It was because of her countless Sunday calls to me, telling me that she loved me and loved the boy we both missed and claimed in our hearts as son and grandson, that I came to treat myself with respect.

Her folded hands in her lap. The news of what I had done now a living thing between us. The silent house. The loss. The pain. The need to say what might heal but could not yet be put into words. We held onto the silence like a wish, she for me and me for her. She, the mother of the child whose child was now our shared ache. The lapse of ten years, knowing he was a boy who lived apart in a life we could not see or reach, an incomprehensible reality. We sat there taking in what could not be changed or rearranged into something that could lift us from our sadness. A day that defined us differently ever after.

I never told my mother that I was sorry. Those were not the words needed, nor would they have been true. Sorry falls short for me. It was irrelevant from the minute I signed the adoption papers. What I am is much deeper and far more complex than sorry can cover. There is no way to adequately describe what it feels like to give up a child. It went against everything I knew and experienced being a child raised on love, as the center of the universe. It goes against everything I have known raising my kids since then. It goes against the grain of my heart, no matter how well I am doing or how much success I have achieved.

Yet, my mother saw in me what she might have been. And I saw in her what I wanted to be and eventually became. A woman who looks to the heart for what remains, long after a sad day is done.

We sat together for a long time on the side of my bed. Me shivering inside her pink bathrobe that I borrowed from the bathroom. My mother with her hands folded on her lap, an image that I cannot erase. The hands that had raised me and loved me were silently clutched in a forced calm.

That day was ten years after my son was born. It took me another twenty to tell my story to my family. I built a protective wall around my heart. A wall that kept my secret safe but also kept others and their kindness out. When I told my family, they did not judge me. Instead, they shared my sadness. Of course, they would have liked to have been there for me, and it grieves them to consider what I endured. But for them to be there, this would have to be a very different story.

I walk among the many who, like me, are birth mothers. I am thankful to have met them and I hope this book will lead me to more. One of my core objectives in writing it is to initiate conversations with other birth mothers. I think of the countless women who have been forced to give up their babies. I have two nieces adopted out of China, and their stories are connected to my own. The loss of their mothers and fathers and their heritage. Somewhere in the vast expanse of China are two women who carried these girls to their birth and then had to give them up, as so many have done there. I think about what the conversation might be among a diverse gathering of birth mothers across nations and circumstances. I want that conversation. I want to shed light on us so that we are seen and heard. It is time to consider the other side of adoption, the women who love our children in their absence.

longing
there is a void
where you should be
a hollow space
that tortures me
I imagine
and conjecture
but I never really know
you
I dream and wait
with an open gate
to my heart
for you
to come home
it has been years
and fears and tears
since I let you go
and still you are
the possible impossible
need in me
for you

the letter

It was a west coast day in Victoria, the kind in which a cold heavy mist blurs the towering fir trees and it seems that the sun might never return. I came out the door with my daughter in a baby jogger, our little dog scampering at the length of his leash that she held tightly in her hand. My infant son was snug inside a carrier on my back. It was just after lunch, and we were headed for the Galloping Goose Trail for our regular afternoon walk, the four of us happy to be outside in the fresh air despite the wet weather. I had often remarked to my mother that, in British Columbia, you could not wait for a sunny day to get outside because it could be a long stretch before one arrived. We took our daily walks, rain or shine, and enjoyed them all.

We set out down the long, steep curve of the driveway, the jogger bumping over the rocky surface, the dog sniffing every twig and bush. I paused at the bottom, checking for traffic on Happy Valley Road, and took a moment to look inside our mailbox. Inside were the usual flyers and bills, and I was about to shut it when I noticed an envelope wedged near the back. I tugged it free, instantly recognizing the address of the Home of the Guardian Angel. I held the envelope, looked at it, felt the cool paper in my hands as I trembled and considered what news it might contain. Such correspondence was infrequent, and it never failed to make me nervous, excited and apprehensive, all at the same time. I looked at this envelope and thought it might hold a response to the letter and photos I had sent via the Home some months prior.

Good news? Any news. I needed news. I felt a rush of hopefulness—maybe it was something more or something better than I imagined. Possibility hung in the air with the rain while my kids waited for me to reconnect with the present and my head and my heart were with the boy I left behind in Halifax. His infant face immediately appeared, along with the complex layers of feelings I had learned to hold in stillness, a practiced calm when I might have otherwise exploded.

I desperately wanted these letters, yet I worried how far down they would take me into that deep well of regret, the dark side of myself I could not reconcile or forgive.

I shook loose from my distraction as my son wriggled inside his carrier. My daughter bounced her heels on the footrest, insisting we go. The dog tugged us all forward. I slipped the mail inside the bottom basket of the jogger, out of the rain. We dashed across the road and entered the green, wet trail.

My daughter chattered to the dog as we made our way down the trail. Usually, I chatted along with my kids, but on this day, I remained quiet, consumed with the envelope and its possibilities. Maybe a message from his mother. I worried that the nuns at the Home had felt the photos I sent in my last letter were inappropriate and were returning them instead of sending them on to my son and his family. A possible rejection. I longed to see what he looked like now. I knew he had brown curly hair and big brown eyes. If he had received the photos of his brother and sister, might he see himself in them? If so, would it make him happy or sad? Would he wish he knew them? Might he resent them and me because they were with me while he was not?

Suddenly my daughter's voice broke through, "Momma!" My son's face was close to mine as I turned to check on him. He was amused, his eyes wide as he watched our little Shih Tzu crisscross the trail, sniffing and marking his territory. All three were buoyantly in the present, and I tried to join them. But I was anxious to finish our walk and had to force my feet to be patient even as my head was racing with questions. I held onto hope, the excitement of what might be inside the envelope. I did my best to respond to my daughter's questions. Soon enough, we came to our turnaround point and headed toward home.

I parked the baby jogger undercover at the front door and unloaded my daughter and the mail. Once inside I sat on the stairs to unhook the baby carrier and pull out my son. I nestled him safely on the wide bottom step of the stairs as we towel dried the dog, removed raincoats, boots and fleece jackets. Then we trekked up the stairs to the kitchen for warm drinks and snacks before snuggling on the couch to read a story before their naps.

Within a half hour, the kids were asleep. I walked back to the kitchen and put the kettle on, knowing I would need a strong cup of tea to steel my courage when I opened the envelope. True to my Newfoundland roots, tea was the remedy I choose for ails and nerves. With the steaming cup on the coffee table, I gently placed the envelope beside it and sat looking at it. Good or bad, the truth of it lay inside. I held onto that for a few minutes, stretching out pleasure and fear, trying not to choose between them. Then, I drew in my breath and opened it.

Inside, there were two items, a letter from the Home's counsellor and a separate envelope on which there was a hand-drawn and pencil-coloured picture of Spiderman. I knew instinctively that my son had drawn and coloured it for me. Inside the decorated envelope was a letter from his mother and a smaller white envelope with "Mary" printed on it—a letter from him. I looked at the Spiderman drawing and, seeing his signature in the corner, I was happy to see the artist in him claim his work. The drawing revealed artistic talent and imagination. I wanted to believe that in this way he was like me—creative, sensitive, expressive. It offered insight into my now twelve-year-old boy, with developing interests and abilities uniquely his own. A boy growing up without me, calling another woman "mother," the woman who helped him prepare the letter. The one who took the time to go to a post office and mail it for him. They might have talked about me. Perhaps she encouraged him to see the good in reaching out to his birth mother, soothing the fears a twelve-year-old might feel when grappling with the confusion of adoption.

I have never been able to let go of the idea that meeting me would be a welcome restoration of the connection between us. The idea that he would look at me and recognize himself gave me an illusion of mother and child becoming as bonded as adoptive mother and child no matter how long we were apart. I kept that secret wish like a smooth stone in my pocket to be touched and warmed and caressed over and over. I held onto it silently while I walked about in my life and whispered, "one day" to myself. "One day."

I read the message from the counsellor first. It contained the usual greetings, hopes that I was well and that I would be pleased with the updates included from his mother and him. It never failed to make me feel awkward and irritated that another person was between us, reading what I sent, what they sent, deciding if the communications were appropriate. I dealt with it and tried to believe it was better than nothing. It was a part of the adoption deal, the relinquishment of personal power.

Next, I read the letter from his mom. She was generous in her news and apologetic for taking so long to respond to my letter and photos. She gave me a snapshot of his life at twelve and told me about his younger sister as well. I wondered then, as I do now, if she felt uncomfortable about providing me with information on the child who is the abiding link between us. We are two versions of mother to him. Mother and birth mother. We are two women forever joined in the story of a boy. Did she hesitate? Did she edit? Did she wonder what I was thinking or wanting? Did I remain a risk that might appear at any time to snatch her comfort and certainty? I hoped not. I wanted her to be my partner in our adoption story and one day invite me into a shared relationship with the boy between us. Yet, I wondered how I would feel if I was in her place. Would I be generous or fiercely protective?

She enclosed two photos of him and one of his younger sister, also adopted. Those photos were the first glimpse I had of him since his birth pictures taken at the hospital, of which I have one. The one that I assume was given to me as a kind of "must do" for the birth mother. Now he was twelve. He was an adolescent with brown curly hair, large brown eyes and a face that showed the beginning of a teenager. He had his birth father's physique and smile. He was, in fact, a perfect blend of the two of us. He had become a boy who wrote me a letter and put my name on the envelope. A boy who drew Spiderman and signed his art with confidence and a flourish.

Taking all of this in, I paused before I opened his letter. I sat looking at my name on the envelope. Mary. That is who I was to him. A woman named Mary who gave birth to him. Gave him up. Lived apart. Had other children. Was absent for the twelve years it took to get to the day when he could write a letter to me. A woman who chose for him to be born but not for herself.

I opened the letter. My heart beating in my ears. My hands shook as I unfolded the page.

I read it quickly. Then again. And again. My heart beating. My tea going cold. Not caring about the tea or the time or the day or anything outside the page that seemed to vibrate with his presence. I am not sure if he wrote the letter entirely on his own as some of the words seemed more formal, more adult, as though someone was helping him say what he wanted to say. The letter was typed, maybe dictated and revised. He spoke of pets and sports and his dad and an uncle.

But then he said something that I have read and reread and wondered about ever since. He said that he felt my pain and sadness. That he felt it too. And that while he was happy in his adoptive family, there was something missing and that something was me. He was happy, yet sad.

Happy, yet sad.

Those three words sum up my existence since the day he was born. More sad than happy a lot of the time. But never one without the other. There have been many times when moments of happiness made me feel guilty. I found it hard to believe I should be allowed to be happy without him. Happy would punch me like a bully's fist putting me back in my place, pushing me down to the dark comfort zone of self-loathing.

What kind of mother gives up a child?

That question sang in the back of my mind and in my core like a dark opera, over and over and over, and never has there been an answer that made sense or released me from the sadness. On joyful days, the claw of regret will reach out and drag me under.

He felt that sadness too, even with the mother, father, happy home and happy life that I had bargained for him in the adoption deal. The sacrifice I made was supposed to guarantee his happiness even as it stole mine. Yet, he felt it. He knew it. He understood the connection with me, that the absence of me held the answer to his sad feelings.

I recalled the night in the nursery when I went to see him and told him how much I loved him. I put everything I had into my touch and words so that he might be imprinted with my love forever. I wished with all my might that it would be so, that despite my absence he would not forget me. That he would feel my love with every heartbeat and every breath. Did my wish come true? If so, I was not sure it had been the right wish because I never intended for him to be sad. Only happy. I never meant to imprint him with my regret.

I put down the letter. The page of black and white. The "Dear Mary." The typed paragraphs. His handwritten signature. The room blurred through tears. The hurt of it, the choice I had made and lived with, descending upon me in my living room on the far west coast of Canada where I was trying to craft a new life, a life that I could say made me happy. The two children sleeping in their beds, so much a part of my heart, who would one day know what I had done. Who would struggle with who I was, and who he was, and why no matter how much I loved them, I still held sadness I could not put aside.

My little dog stirred on the couch, stretching his legs and then relaxing back into dreams. It was raining in earnest outside, making the mid-afternoon dark and gloomy. My tea had gone cold. I thought to make another cup. I knew the kids would be waking up soon, so I needed to put everything away and get ready for them. I took one last look at the photos. I smiled at him as he smiled out from the pictures, school photos cut from a sheet. Then I placed them inside the Spiderman envelope. I sat holding the envelope for a few minutes before I got up and took it to my bedroom to place in the box where I kept his baby photo and previous letters from the Home. A small treasure trove of him to be taken out and enjoyed when I had privacy and the courage to endure the inevitable rush of emotions.

It felt wrong to keep his things in a box. His photos sealed away where they could not be seen. It was the secret of him and the lie about me. He was my son. I was his mother. Now he was adopted, and I was living as though he did not exist. To the world, I was the mother of two, not three. He was growing up and becoming his own person. He was already old enough to articulate his feelings about me being the missing part of his life. He became even more real to me. More tangible.

I walked back out into the quiet of the house and stood staring out at the rain. As had been the case so many times in my life, I was alone as the truth, the only truth that mattered, gripped my heart. That boy in the photos was mine, but not mine. I wrestled with the tug between those two opposites knowing I could never escape their parallel existence within me. He was a boy in the photos but not a boy who would come bursting through my door calling out to me as he clamoured up the stairs to tell me about his day. That belonged to someone else and had since he was two weeks old.

It was the everyday that was lost. Watching him grow and change. Seeing him crawl and then walk. Reading to him. Teaching him to read. Kissing him goodnight. Tucking him into bed. Soothing him when he was sick or sad or hurt. Watching movies on the couch while we ate popcorn, nestled under a blanket. Decorating Christmas trees. Being silly. Laughing until our sides hurt. Blowing out birthday candles. Hunting for Easter eggs. Skipping rocks across the water. Taking walks on summer evenings. Shopping for shoes and smart-looking clothes. Teasing him about girls. Surprising him with presents, just because. Wiping his tears. Understanding his fears. Believing in his dreams. Watching him become his own person. Saying I love you, thousands of times. Thousands and thousands of times. And letting love be enough to sustain us. Those things and so many more were lost.

I turned from the window to see my daughter toddling out of her room, rubbing sleep from her eyes. She came towards me with arms outstretched, and I picked her up and held her tightly. The warmth and realness of her overcame me. Sensing my emotions, she pulled back and looked into my eyes. My daughter could read me well, even then. She kissed my cheek, and I kissed her back. I was happy, in the midst of sad, as we walked together into her brother's room to wake him from his nap.

That was my eldest son's single letter to me. I continued to write to the Home over the years. I telephoned and spoke to counsellors. Whenever I moved, I kept my contact information up to date with them in case he or his mother sent more letters. The counsellors urged me to be patient. They told me that he would reach out to me when he was ready. "Boys take longer," they explained. "Most get curious about their biological parents once they have children of their own." That seemed an impossible amount of time. Unendurable time, lived one day after another, without knowing when or if.

No letters appeared. There was only the long, slow, empty roar of silence.

Eventually, I convinced myself that it was in his best interest that I leave him alone. My presence would be confusing. I had given him up to the care of his parents, and while I was his birth mother, I was not his mother. I had no claim to him. It was better that I let him decide when he wanted to find me. I submitted my contact information to the Nova Scotia Registry when he turned nineteen and, once again, to the Home to relay to him. When he was ready, he could easily find me.

More and more years went by, and still, I believed that it was right and best for me to wait, to let him decide. When I doubted myself, I called the Home, and they reaffirmed that I was doing the right thing.

I did not get good at waiting. I am still not good at it. I endure it. There is not a Mother's Day or a birthday of his that I don't wake up thinking, "Maybe today."

There were long periods when I have not looked at the letter or the pictures. I could not take them out. It was too painful to see him and know that the twelve-year-old boy was now a teenager, a young man, a man. When I do unbox them, I am always alone, and I give myself permission to cry and be as sad as I need to be, as sad as I am. It's a solitary, private admission of regret and loss and heartbreak. I hold the paper and close my eyes, trying to feel him. Trying to know him, even if just a little. The page and the photos quiver between my fingers, allowing me to convince myself that he is in them. But I realize, every time, that it is me that quivers. It is my own hands that long for the touch of him so badly that I am willing to believe the page and the picture hold him.

It may be, as he said, that I am the something that is missing in his life even as he is the something, someone, missing in mine. Perhaps even after all these years, he is aware of me between the details of his everyday. In his quiet moments, I may resonate in the constant beat of his heart that for nine months beat along with mine. Surely, if there is a God, and I believe there is, she lets that kind of memory stay within us no matter what comes after. Perhaps that is how I have been gifted with the strength to wait, and the courage to believe that I do not wait in vain.

what if

I love you

for a lifetime

but you

never know my love

a love sent

but not received

or believed

to be real

a love

that might heal

if you

let it in

between us

oh my darling

the what if

stays upon me

as

I

wait

for

you

the end is not the end

Here we are at the last chapter, and I have not yet met my son. I dreamed about writing about our reunion here. In my imagination, I compose many versions of that ending and find comfort in them. They are with me on sleepless nights and when I tell my story to others. They are the endings that keep me hopeful and encouraged.

I found him. It was so easy to do that it made the years of waiting seem wasted. The answer had been right in front of me.

Writing this book encouraged me to initiate contact, to bring him into the story that is his as well as mine. I was inspired by other birth mothers who had found their children and built relationships with them.

In January of 2017, I sorted once again through the box that contains everything I have related to my son. The letter he wrote to me when he was twelve arrived with no return address and didn't include his last name, but now I realized he'd mentioned the name of a relative in Vancouver. I stared at the name and thought that, with social media, I might be able to track him down. I opened my laptop, signed into Facebook—and found him within a few minutes. I wrote a message explaining who I was and that I was searching for my son. I read the message several times over before I pressed the send button, then got up from my desk and went into the kitchen to prepare dinner. I set my iPhone on the table, wondering if I would hear anything back. My phone pinged with a message. The person responding asked me a few identifying questions and several messages later confirmed that he was the person I was seeking.

It was a glorious, joyful moment. I danced and cried. I immediately threw myself into every previously imagined version of meeting my son. I imagined myself on a plane, flying across Canada to see him. I was picking outfits and planning what to bring him—photos and presents and my book draft. I was sure that the interminable years of waiting were at an end. I believed my 1983 deal with God that my son would be returned to me one day was coming true at last. I thanked my deceased mother, believing she had a part in what was happening. The thought of her and how much she wanted me to find my son, her grandson, left me in a mess of sobbing gratefulness. I told her how sorry I was that I had not found him while she was still alive. Those first few moments were a storm of emotions.

I called my husband at work and burst out my news. He came swiftly home, bearing flowers, and enfolded me in his warm hug. There is no way to describe just how jubilant I was. He let me chatter on about every detail and plan. I could not think of anything else but the happy ending that was so close I could touch it. I was delirious. It was what I had dreamed of, wanted and waited for.

My husband let me go on and on. Only after I had finally calmed down a bit did he pull me to him to say that I needed to be prepared for the possibility that my son might not want to meet me. I was unwilling to let that in. I heard what he was saying, but he had to be wrong. I needed him to be wrong.

He was not.

Less than twenty-four hours later, my joy was flattened. My son's adoptive mother wrote to say she did not think he would want to meet me. There had been difficult teenage years that she and her now ex-husband had to love and support him through. He had suffered and was angry about being adopted. In the space of a few paragraphs, my dreamed-of ending was obliterated. The euphoria was gone, replaced with crushing disappointment.

I was angry. I was ripped apart. I wanted to scream and tell her that this was not acceptable or possible. I wanted to tell her to get the hell out of my way and let me talk to my son. MY son! She had to be wrong. Where did she get off thinking that he would not want to meet me? Why was she making me go through her?

I let myself come apart before I could return to reason. I fought my way back from dark anger to a place where I could accept, once more, that I am not his mother. I gave up that right. That's what adoption means. She is his mother. Not me. And he has the right to refuse me. Now and for good, if he chooses. Whatever deal I made with God is null and void for as long as my son wants it that way.

The good news is that he is now married with children and they are doing well. Within a couple of weeks of that initial email, a second email from his mother confirmed that he did not want contact. That moment, those words, took me down once more, but this time I was prepared. This was the outcome of giving him up. The one I had not ever believed would be true yet was.

My husband encouraged me to look at the positive—that little baby I chose to give up so he could have the best possible life is now an adult who is well, happy, married and has children. These were all things that I hoped would be true for him. My husband reminded me that it was not "no" but rather "not now." Slowly, I came to find comfort in those things. I know my husband is right. My son's life is going well, and he is busy raising young children. Letting me in might feel like a risk, something that might unsettle his hard-won, happy world. He might not be ready to go back to the pain associated with me, the woman who gave him up.

I know little of what happened when he was a teenager except that it was a difficult period for him. I have been reading a series called "Dear Adoption," in which adoptees disclose their struggles with being adopted. There are unanswered questions, unexplainable feelings of a void, and the resounding, often concealed, hurt of not being with their natural parents and family. There is a loss of identity and the historical context of who they are. There are the constant "why" and "why not" and "why me" questions that interfere with belonging and adopted familial connections. There are so many loose ends that never quite knit together, no matter how much they are loved and nurtured in their adopted family.

Adoption is an unnatural separation of mother and child. There are biological connections. There are shared characteristics: the curl of our hair, the colour of our eyes. The sound of our laughter or how we hold our heads when considering a thought, or our similar inclination for sadness and anger. I have often wondered if he likes to read as I do.

Might we share the same taste in music and irresistible urge to dance? Do people remark on his smile as so many do mine? Is he sentimental? Does he run? Does he eat well and take care of his health?

I wonder again how I could have let him go. I am stopped and strangled by what I did. It comes in waves, more frequent now that I have learned how deeply he was affected. He suffered. I am responsible for that. No matter what anyone says, I am responsible.

At twenty-two, I earnestly believed that giving him a life of two parents, a home and security mattered more than what I could have offered him. I wanted to protect him and did what I did because I thought it was best for him. What I did not see was that, in the process, I was also depriving him. Depriving him of my love. And even though I kept on loving him, it was a distant love. In my absence, he could not see or feel that I love him and that giving him up was about that love. I told myself that we would somehow stay connected across the miles, that he would feel me out here waiting for him.

I gave up my child. His mother described it as a gift that I had given them. I know what she meant, but gift is too small a word to describe giving up a baby.

I gave them a part of me. A boy with ten perfect fingers and ten perfect toes and rosy cheeks. A boy with the imprint of me on his heart. A boy who I have lived without and missed and longed for and died a thousand deaths of regret.

That is not just a gift. It is a sacrifice. He was my heart and soul, my flesh and blood. And he is still.

I am certain much was right in his life, and he was and is well loved. But I believe now that my absence was an ever-present factor for him.

Just as is true for me of missing him, no one and nothing could make up for the lack of me in his life. It could not be filled by any measure of happiness or success. What I wait for now is for him to remember what he wrote to me when he was twelve. He said, "There is something missing in my life. I believe it is you." That void is the one undeniable thing that connects us. It is what I hope will eventually lead us back to one another. We will never restore what has been missed, but we can make a future shaped by an us that chooses love over loss, hope over despondency, and heart over hurt.

I spent these recent years trying to ready myself for when we meet. I wanted him to see me as a remarkable woman. I wanted to be a person he would be proud to call his birth mother. I overcame the failings of my past and created a worthwhile life. I am now married to a man who is my equal and my true love. I am a confident woman. I know myself and live on my terms. I have the respect and admiration of many.

I am ready.

He is not.

I stand in my sadness, and then force myself to find my positive, hopeful self—the me who believes that when the time comes, when he is ready, it will be the best and right time.

If he chooses not to meet me, ever, this book will still be his. In it, he will find me, the girl-woman-mother who gave him life. I hope that, in finding me, in person or on the page, the void will be at last be filled with the certainty that he was born out of love. He always was and always will be loved by me.

The end is not the end. I choose to believe in my versions of a happy ending, imagined and dreamed. They will continue to sustain me.

Until ...

acknowledgement

To Matthew, my son who was raised by another mother. Our nine months and few minutes together changed me profoundly and are deeply woven into every good thing in my life, despite the aching loss I've felt every day since leaving you with another family. I'll never stop being grateful for your presence in my life, even if that presence can only be in my heart.

I am grateful to many people who have supported me as I brought my book to life. They are:

My mother, who we sadly lost in 2016. She consistently, lovingly and persistently urged me to write my story. I did it, Mom! I think you would be proud. This book is my effort to honour you as my mother and as the grandmother of the boy you never knew but loved with your whole heart.

My children Ben and Rebecca, for your patience with me as I unravelled my truth in front of you, with you and for you, so that you might see me as I am, flawed and real and unswervingly in love with you. The trauma of adoption has affected us all, I know, but the blessing in that loss is I have never once taken for granted the privilege of raising you. You two make my world a beautiful place.

My husband, Blaine. Your unwavering support for my writing, which stayed true through my bouts of emotional turmoil and dark moments of wanting to give up, was my core of calm and love. Without you, this book would still be a dream and a wish. You are my darling and my dearest.

My family. The best family a girl could have—no judgement, only love. Your kindness, generosity and unfailing support are unequalled. A special note to my sister, Michelle, who believes in my writing, shares the adoption story with me and who travelled down under with me to Australia on the Oprah adventure that changed us both for the better.

Megan Watts, my publisher. When you walked into my life that first evening, I knew instantly that I had found my perfect partner to get my book into print. Megan, your positive light and take-action approach propelled me forward. You are a light in the world. A joy and a publisher powerhouse queen!

Lori Bamber, my editor, for whom I find it hard to find words to properly wrap around my gratitude. Your wisdom, grace, clarity and loving care of my words and my story allowed me to take what I had written to its best form. I adore you. I cherish our conversations and all that you offered me. Namaste.

Laura Wrubleski, my graphic designer. You looked into my story and drew out the design for the cover and it was as if you read my heart. You saw me and knew me and visually captured my story.

My circle of women friends. Your unending encouragement buoyed me in our times together and in the long days of writing when I needed your words to lift me. Each of you inspire me and I am thankful every day to claim my place beside you in the world.

So many of us have a powerful testimony
about surviving the fires of loss, trauma and
shame. Perhaps we all do. And each time
someone frees themselves, we are all a little
more capable of freedom.

Perhaps our stories are similar. Perhaps not.
Whatever your story is, I urge you to let your
fierce soul step fully into the arena of life.
Believe that your path was meant to bring
you here. Tell your story. Own it. Be brave
and bold, and by doing so, help others
find their way.